IRRESISTIBLE
EMAILS

A Neuro-Marketing Guide to
Writing Emails That Convert

Vince Warnock

ATG
PUBLISHING

For information contact :

ATG Publishing

info@atgpublishing.com - http://www.atgpublishing.com

ISBN: 9781991123091

First Edition: November 2024

10 9 8 7 6 5 4 3 2 1

Contents

Contents 3

Dedication 9

Introduction... 13

What Are Email Nurture Sequences, Anyway? 14

Why Should You Care?... 15

Understanding Your Audience 17

Buyer Personas.. 17

Customer Journey Mapping: Following the Yellow Brick
Road 21

Segmentation Strategies: No More One-Size-Fits-All 25

Setting Clear Goals 29

Defining Objectives 29

Key Performance Indicators (KPIs) 31

Setting SMART Goals 32

Planning Your Sequence 35

How Many Emails? The Goldilocks Principle.................... 35

Timing is Everything: When to Hit Send 37

Content Mapping: The Right Message at the Right Time 38

Crafting Compelling Subject Lines 41

Psychological Triggers: Pushing Those Brain Buttons.........42

A/B Testing Strategies: May the Best Subject Line Win........53

Avoiding Spam Filters: Stay Out of Email Jail.......................55

Subject Line Formulas: Your Secret Sauce 56

The Preview Text: Your Subject Line's Sidekick 59

Writing Engaging Email Content 63

Storytelling Techniques: Once Upon a Time in Email Land.63

Personalization and Dynamic Content: Make It All About
Them...65

Neuro-Linguistic Programming (NLP) Principles: Jedi Mind
Tricks for Emails 67

The Art of Persuasion: Creating Genuine Influence in Email
Communications..69

Optimizing Email Structure for Modern Readers 71

Crafting Effective Calls-to-Action: Driving Meaningful
Engagement 73

The P.S. Is Your Secret Weapon...74

Creating Balance in Email Communications.........................75

Email Design Principles 77

Mobile-First Design Strategy 77

Visual Hierarchy: Guide Their Eyes Like A Pro 79

Color Psychology: Painting Emotions with Your Palette 81

Typography: Font-astic Ways to Capture Attention.............83

Images and Graphics: Worth a Thousand Words (If You Use Them Right)..85

The Power of Plain Text: When Simple Emails Make Strategic Sense...87

Maintaining Visual Consistency in Email Communications.89

Accessibility: Design for Everyone 91

Effective Calls-to-Action...95

Strategic Positioning...95

Design: Make It Pop!...97

Crafting Compelling CTA Language.........................99

Creating Urgency and Scarcity: The Fear of Missing Out (FOMO) Factor 101

Reducing Friction: Make It Easy to Say Yes.........................103

Personalization: Make It All About Them...........................105

Neuro-Marketing and Cognitive Bias in Emails 107

The Reciprocity Principle: Give and You Shall Receive 108

Social Proof: Everybody's Doing It.........................110

Loss Aversion: 112

The Zeigarnik Effect: The Power of Unfinished Business...114

The Framing Effect: It's All About Perspective 116

The Anchoring Effect: Setting the Right Reference Point ..118

The Paradox of Choice: Less Can Be More 120

The Commitment and Consistency Principle: Small Yeses
Lead to Big Yeses..122

Automation and Personalization 125

Trigger-Based Emails: Right Message, Right Time 125

Behavioral Segmentation: Because Actions Speak Louder
Than Words 127

Dynamic Content: One Email, Many Versions.....................128

Personalization Beyond {FirstName}...................................130

Automation Workflows: Building Your Email Marketing
Machine 132

The Human Touch in Automation: Keeping It Real............133

Compliance and Best Practices 137

Staying on the Right Side of the Law (and Your Subscribers)
....137

Practical Implementation 139

Double Opt-In: The Gold Standard of Consent...................139

List Hygiene: Keeping Your Email List Squeaky Clean 142

Managing Unsubscribes and Preferences...........................144

Privacy and Data Protection: Treating Subscriber Data Like
Fort Knox 147

Deliverability Best Practices: Staying Out of the Spam Folder

.... 150

Advanced Techniques 155

Taking Your Email Game to the Next Level 155

Interactive Emails: Bringing the Web to the Inbox 155

Gamification in Email Marketing: Let's Play! 159

Integrating Email with Other Channels: Breaking Down the
Silos 162

User-Generated Content (UGC) in Emails: Let Your
Customers Do the Talking 165

Where to From Here (and How to Stay Ahead of the Curve).. 169

Key Takeaways 170

Staying Ahead of the Curve: Your Email Marketing Growth
Plan 172

About the Author 177

More Books by Vince Warnock 179

Dedication

To Leanne, my rock and my adventure buddy—no one makes life better than you do.

To Oriana and Jarvis, no longer kids, you are both my greatest joy.

To Jess, and Q, for always having my back and being my constant source of motivation. I couldn't do it without you. I wish everyone had friends as good as you.

And to Olivia, whose endless questions and love for the unknown gave life to this book. You're one of a kind!

Special Promo - Take Your Email Marketing to the Next Level!

Loved what you've learned so far? Ready to put it into action and master the art of irresistible emails?

Join our exclusive 15-day email course and learn step-by-step how to craft emails that captivate, convert, and build lasting connections. Whether you're just starting out or looking to refine your skills, this course will guide you through everything you need to know to create emails that stand out.

For just $39 USD, you'll receive:

- Daily bite-sized lessons with actionable exercises
- Insider strategies for subject lines, automation, personalization, and more
- Proven techniques to boost engagement and drive results

Scan the QR Code to Get Started!

https://chasingtheinsights.com/15-days-to-master-email-marketing/

Introduction

Welcome to the world of advanced email nurture sequences. My goal with this book is to take you on a journey of exploration. I want to show you how to transform your email marketing strategy by incorporating neuro-marketing techniques, thereby creating campaigns that resonate deeply with your audience and drive meaningful results.

Email nurture sequences can represent a sophisticated approach to customer communication. Rather than isolated messages, these sequences offer a carefully orchestrated journey, guiding subscribers from initial interest to loyal advocacy. When executed effectively, they act as a virtual brand ambassador, delivering the right message at the right time, tailored to each subscriber's needs and preferences.

However, we're taking this concept a step further. By integrating neuro-marketing principles, we'll delve into the psychology behind consumer behavior and decision-making processes. This approach allows us to craft emails that not only inform and engage but also trigger specific cognitive responses, enhancing the overall impact of our communications.

Throughout this book, we'll cover a wide range of topics, including:

- The fundamentals of effective email nurture sequences
- Key neuro-marketing concepts and their application in email marketing
- Strategies for mapping customer journeys and aligning content accordingly
- Techniques for personalizing emails based on psychological profiles
- Methods for using neuro-marketing insights to optimize subject lines, content, and calls-to-actions

Whether your goal is to welcome new subscribers, nurture leads, re-engage dormant customers, or drive sales, this book provides you with the knowledge and tools to elevate your email marketing strategy.

What Are Email Nurture Sequences, Anyway?

Think of an email nurture sequence as a series of thoughtfully crafted messages that land in your subscriber's inbox at just the right time. It's like having a conversation with each of your customers, but way more scalable (and you don't have to remember everyone's name).

These sequences are designed to:

- Show subscribers the ropes (aka educate them about what you offer)
- Build trust (because nobody likes a pushy salesperson)
- Answer those "but what if..." questions before they're even asked
- Keep your brand on their mind (in a good way, not a stalker-ish way)
- Gently nudge them towards taking action (whether that's making a purchase, signing up for a demo, or simply engaging more with your content)

Why Should You Care?

Let's face it, everyone's inbox seems to be bursting at the seams; standing out is tougher than ever. That's where nurture sequences come to the rescue. Here's why they're a big deal:

They're personal: No more "Dear Valued Customer" nonsense. We're talking tailor-made content that makes your subscribers feel special.

They do the work for you: Set 'em up once, and they'll keep nurturing leads while you sleep. It's like having a marketing team who never takes a coffee break.

They're conversion machines: By building relationships over time, you're more likely to turn subscribers into happy customers.

They're budget-friendly: Once you've got your sequence running, it's a low-cost way to keep your marketing engine humming.

They're data goldmines: Each email gives you insights into what makes your audience tick.

They keep your brand voice consistent: No more Jekyll and Hyde marketing messages.

They're in it for the long haul: These sequences help you build lasting relationships, not just one-time sales.

Throughout this book, we'll unpack all the secrets to creating nurture sequences that will make your subscribers look forward to hearing from you. Whether you're just starting out, or you're looking to level up your email game, we've got you covered.

Understanding Your Audience

Before we start crafting those killer nurture sequences, we need to talk about the stars of the show – your audience. After all, you wouldn't buy a birthday gift without knowing the recipient, right? The same goes for email marketing. Let's break down how to really get to know your subscribers. As I wrote that, I realized there's an exception to this. I used to work in a corporate office and hated that time of the year where we all had to get Secret Santa gifts...I can assure you that I rarely made an effort to get to know the recipient before buying a stock-standard Secret Santa gift.

Buyer Personas

First, let's do a little exercise in imagination (don't worry, it's totally professional). We're going to create buyer personas—detailed profiles of your ideal customers. Think of it like creating characters for your marketing story. These personas are key to understanding who you're trying to reach and how best to communicate with them. Just like a well-developed character in a novel, a well-crafted persona will help you tailor your message in a way that resonates with your audience. By getting into the mindset of your ideal customer, you'll be better equipped to address their needs, solve their problems, and make your marketing efforts truly effective. So let's dive in and bring these personas to life—this will guide everything from your tone of voice to the kind of offers that appeal to your audience.

To build effective buyer personas:

Analyze customer data

Take a close look at customer data, surveys, and analytics to understand what drives your customers and what they're looking for. Use tools like Google Analytics, CRM data, and social media insights to gather as much information as possible. This will help identify trends and behaviors that are essential for shaping your personas.

Understand the customers' needs

A good persona isn't just about basic demographics—it's about deeply understanding needs and motivations. The more you understand what they care about, the stronger your persona will be. Consider what problems your product or service solves for the customer, what goals they have, and what challenges they face.

Knowing customers' pain points allows you to craft more meaningful messages that resonate with them.

Identify patterns

Look for common behaviors, preferences, and challenges that many of your customers share. Finding these patterns will enable you to create personas that accurately reflect your audience. Group customers by similar traits such as buying habits, product preferences, or engagement levels. This allows you to gain insight into how different segments of your audience think and behave.

Create visual representations

Give each persona a name and pick a representative image. This makes the persona feel real and relatable to your team. Adding details such as age, occupation, and hobbies can further humanize the persona. Visual elements make it easier for everyone involved in marketing and sales to connect with these personas on a personal level.

Construct detailed stories

Describe the personas daily routines, main concerns, and strengths. Adding these details brings the persona to life and provides more context for how to reach them. Think about their typical day—what activities they do, what decisions they make, and how your product fits into their life. This storytelling approach will help you identify the best times and ways to communicate with them.

Validate with real examples

Compare your personas with real customer profiles to ensure they're accurate and relevant. Use interviews, focus groups, and feedback from customer-facing teams to ensure your personas match actual customer behaviors. This validation step keeps your personas grounded in reality, avoiding assumptions that do not align with real-world data.

Update regularly

Adjust your personas as you gather new information to keep them useful and reflective of any changes in your audience. Customer preferences and behaviors can evolve over time; it's important to revisit your personas periodically. Regular updates ensure marketing remains targeted and effective, even as your audience shifts.

Remember, these personas aren't real people, but they should feel real. The more detailed and relatable they are, the more helpful they will be!

Make sure to share your personas with your entire team so that everyone has a clear understanding of who your target customers are, and how to best serve them. The more aligned your team is, the more cohesive your marketing efforts will be.

Customer Journey Mapping: Following the Yellow Brick Road

Now, let's map out the journey your customers take—from the moment they think, "Who are you?" to the point where they say, "I can't live without you!" This is super important to ensure your nurture sequence hits at just the right time.

To create an effective customer journey map:

Define key stages

Break down the main phases of the customer journey. Usually, this includes stages such as Awareness (when customers first learn about you), Consideration (when they're deciding if they want your product), Decision (when they choose to buy), and Post-Purchase (after they've bought your product).

You might also consider adding other stages that are relevant to your business, such as Onboarding (where customers learn how to use your product) or Loyalty (when customers become repeat buyers and advocates). Through defining these stages, you understand where customers are, and how to move them forward.

Identify interaction points

Figure out where and how customers interact with your brand at each stage. Some examples are through social media, emails, website visits, and conversations with your sales team.

By mapping out these touchpoints you will understand which channels are most effective and where there may be gaps. Interaction points might include reading a blog post, watching a video, visiting a landing page, and reaching out for customer support. The more detailed you are, the better you'll be able to address each customer's needs.

Analyze emotional states

Think about the potential emotions customers could feel at each point—curiosity when they first find out about you, uncertainty when they're weighing options, enthusiasm when they decide to buy, or satisfaction after they've made a purchase.

Understanding these emotions allows you to create messaging that resonates. For instance, during the Awareness stage, you might focus on sparking curiosity and excitement, while during the Consideration stage, you'll want to alleviate concerns and doubts.

Emotional mapping enables you to create empathetic content that speaks directly to what your customers are feeling.

Locate opportunities

Find places where your nurture sequence can step in to solve problems, provide helpful information, and make the experience even better. Look for areas where customers potentially need a little more reassurance or motivation.

For example, if customers are hesitating during the Decision stage, this might be a great opportunity to send a testimonial or a case study to build confidence. Identifying these moments means you can be proactive in helping your customers continue their journey without obstacles.

Align content strategy

Create targeted content for each stage that meets the specific needs and emotions of your customers. For example, provide informative content during the Awareness stage, and reassurance during the Decision stage.

Content takes many forms—blog posts, videos, infographics, webinars, and even customer testimonials. The key is to ensure that the content matches where the customer is in their journey, and addresses what they need at that moment. Personalized content that speaks directly to their challenges and goals makes a big difference in engagement.

Measure and refine

Set up ways to track how well your journey map is working. Use customer feedback and data to make improvements over time. Metrics like open rates, click-through rates, conversion rates, and customer satisfaction scores provide valuable insights into how well your journey map is performing. Don't be afraid to make changes based on what you learn—effective customer journey mapping is an ongoing process.

Regularly revisiting and refining your journey map keeps it relevant, ensuring your marketing efforts are in tune with your customers' evolving needs.

Think of this journey map as your treasure map to keeping customers happy—and driving conversions!

It's not just a static plan, but a living tool that evolves alongside your customers. The better you understand the journey they take, the better you can serve them—and ultimately turn them into loyal advocates for your brand.

Segmentation Strategies: No More One-Size-Fits-All

Now let's talk about segmentation. This is how you avoid being the person who sends cat videos to friends who prefer dogs. By segmenting your email list, you can make sure your messages are relevant and meaningful to each group of subscribers.

Segmentation allows you to better understand customer needs, providing a personalized experience. When you tailor your messages to fit the preferences of specific groups, you improve engagement, boost open rates, and build stronger relationships with your audience. It's all about sending the right message to the right people at the right time, making your subscribers feel understood and valued.

Here are some simple ways to segment your email list:

Demographics

Group people by age, location, job title, or other basic characteristics. This helps you tailor your content to fit different lifestyles and needs. For example, you can send location-specific promotions or target messages based on a recipient's career stage.

Behavior

Look at what subscribers have done in the past—what emails they've clicked on, what products they've bought, or what they've ignored. Use this information to create personalized campaigns reflecting their behavior. For instance, if someone frequently clicks on sale emails, prioritize sending them discounts or exclusive offers.

Engagement level

Separate the highly engaged subscribers—your super fans—from those who haven't been interacting much. This lets you reward your biggest supporters while re-engaging those who might need a nudge. High-engagement segments can receive exclusive perks, while less active subscribers might benefit from re-engagement campaigns with incentives to boost interest.

Purchase history

Segment your email list by purchase behavior, like first-time buyers, repeat customers, big spenders, or deal hunters. This lets you craft messages that match buying habits, such as welcoming new customers and rewarding loyal ones. For example, offer a loyalty discount to regular buyers or a special welcome offer to encourage first-time buyers to come back and make their next purchase.

Interests

Group subscribers based on the topics or product categories they love. If someone constantly clicks on fitness content, send them more of that. The goal is to focus on what they care about most. By understanding their interests, you can make emails feel highly relevant, increasing the chances of engagement and action.

Needs and Motivations

Think about what outcome your product or service fulfills for the subscriber. What gap are they trying to fill? By understanding this you are able to target your messaging directly to their needs. For instance, if your product helps people save time, focus your messaging on the time-saving benefits for subscribers whose main challenge is a busy schedule.

Lifecycle stage

Segment the email list based on where subscribers are in their journey with your brand. New subscribers, long-time customers, and those who are close to churn require different messaging. Understanding their lifecycle stage enables you to send appropriate messages to nurture each group effectively—such as onboarding information for new subscribers or win-back incentives for those who are becoming disengaged.

Preferences

Allow subscribers to set preferences for content type and frequency. Some may prefer educational content, while others are looking for promotions or updates. Giving them control over what they receive leads to higher satisfaction and lower unsubscribe rates.

The main goal of segmentation is to create groups that you can speak to in a more personal way. Let's be honest, we all like to feel special—and the more personal your emails are, the better the connection with your audience.

Remember, understanding your audience is an ongoing process. Keep listening, learning, and adjusting your approach to keep your segments relevant and your messages effective.

With a deep understanding of your audience in place, we can move on to the crucial step of planning the email nurture sequence. This next phase is key to making sure your campaign is effective. In the next section, we'll look at how to set clear, measurable goals for email sequences, ensuring that each email serves a purpose and helps guide recipients along their customer journey. Let's dive into this essential step to craft a successful email marketing strategy.

Setting Clear Goals

Having established a clear understanding of our target audience, the next crucial task is to define the objectives of our email nurture sequence. Setting precise goals is akin to charting a course for a journey; without a clear destination, our efforts may lack direction and efficiency. This step is essential in ensuring that each element of our sequence contributes meaningfully to the overall marketing strategy, optimizing resources and maximizing the impact of our campaign.

Defining Objectives

To begin, it's crucial to clearly define the primary objectives of your nurture sequence. Consider these potential goals:

Engagement: Increase open rates, read-through rates, and click-through rates to enhance overall interaction with your content.

Conversion: Transform prospective customers into active buyers of your product or service.

Retention: Maintain customer satisfaction and loyalty, reducing churn rates.

Education: Develop subscribers' knowledge, potentially turning them into informed advocates for your brand.

Upselling: Encourage existing customers to upgrade to premium or complementary offerings.

While it's possible to pursue multiple objectives, it's advisable to identify a primary goal. Ensure that any secondary objectives align with and support your main aim.

Pro tip: Be specific! Instead of "increase sales," aim for a precise target such as "increase sales of our premium package by 15% among first-time buyers within the next quarter." This level of detail facilitates accurate measurement and evaluation of your sequence's success.

Key Performance Indicators (KPIs)

Now that we know what we're aiming for, how do we know if we're hitting the bullseye? Enter KPIs - the metrics that'll tell you if your nurture sequence is crushing it or needs a timeout.

Here are some KPIs to consider, depending on your goals:

Open rates: Are your subject lines irresistible clickbait (in a good way)?

Click-through rates (CTR): Are people actually engaging with your content?

Conversion rates: Are your calls-to-action (CTAs) working their magic?

Revenue per email: How much money is each email bringing in?

List growth rate: Is your subscriber family growing? Unsubscribe rate: Are people breaking up with you? (It happens to the best of us)

Customer Lifetime Value (CLV): Are your nurture sequences turning one-time buyers into lifelong fans?

Choose three to five KPIs that align with your objectives. These will be your North Star, guiding strategy and helping measure success.

Setting SMART Goals

Let's take those objectives and KPIs and turn them into SMART goals.

SMART stands for:

Specific: Nail down exactly what you want to achieve.
Measurable: Make sure you can track your progress.
Achievable: Be ambitious while keeping it real.
Relevant: Align with your overall marketing and business goals.
Time-bound: Set a deadline to keep yourself accountable.

Here's an example:

"Increase our email-driven sales by 20% in the next quarter by implementing a 5-email nurture sequence for new subscribers, achieving a 25% open rate and a 10% click-through rate."

Now that's a SMART goal! It gives a clear target to aim for and a way to measure success.

Remember, your goals might evolve as you learn more about your audience and what resonates with them. That's okay! The important thing is to start with a clear direction and be ready to adjust your compass along the way.

Having established clear objectives, we have laid a solid

foundation for developing an effective nurture sequence. The following section will focus on the strategic planning of a campaign.

We will explore crucial elements such as determining the optimal number of emails, identifying the most effective timing for each communication, and curating content that resonates with the audience at each stage of their journey. This comprehensive approach will enable you to construct a well-structured and impactful email marketing strategy.

Planning Your Sequence

As we proceed to the planning phase of the nurture sequence, it's essential to approach this process with strategic precision. Consider this stage as crafting a carefully orchestrated journey for your subscribers, where each touchpoint is thoughtfully placed to guide them effectively towards your desired outcome. The objective is to create a seamless progression that engages and informs at appropriate intervals, avoiding potential disengagement. In this section of the book, we will examine the key components of this process.

How Many Emails? The Goldilocks Principle

Determining the optimal number of emails in your sequence requires a balanced approach:

Begin with a standard framework: A typical nurture sequence often consists of 5-7 emails. However, this guideline should be adjusted based on your specific circumstances.

Align with objectives: Goals should influence the sequence length. Educational campaigns may require more touchpoints, while conversion-focused sequences benefit from brevity.

Consider audience characteristics: Tailor the frequency to your audience's preferences and habits. High-level executives appreciate concise communication, while enthusiasts could engage with extensive content.

Monitor and adjust strategically: Begin with your planned email cadence and analyze performance metrics. Reduce frequency if engagement declines, or expand the sequence when metrics indicate sustained audience interest. This data-driven approach ensures sequences remain optimally aligned with subscriber behavior.

It's crucial to prioritize quality over quantity. A sequence of fewer, high-impact emails proves more effective than a longer series of less compelling messages.

Timing is Everything: When to Hit Send

The timing of email sequences is super important, significantly influencing its success. Consider these key elements when determining your deployment strategy:

Email Frequency: The optimal cadence varies based on your campaign objectives and audience characteristics:

Welcome Sequences: Initialize with daily emails, gradually reducing frequency

Sales-Focused Campaigns: Alternate-day deployments often prove effective

Long-Term Nurture Programs: Maintain engagement with weekly or bi-weekly communications

Deployment Timing: While no universal optimal sending time exists, consider testing unconventional scheduling. When most organizations concentrate their email deployment at traditional times (such as Tuesday at 10 AM), alternative timing (such as Sunday evenings, or Tuesdays at 7:05 AM) may yield higher engagement rates

Trigger Mechanisms: Implement a strategic combination of:

Time-Based Triggers: Schedule emails at predetermined intervals following specific events

Behavior-Based Triggers: Deploy emails in response to subscriber actions

This balanced approach to timing ensures the sequence maintains consistent engagement and avoids audience fatigue.

Content Mapping: The Right Message at the Right Time

Here's where we align your email content with the subscriber's journey. It's like being a mind reader, but way less creepy.

Your email nurture sequence should feel like a natural conversation that evolves with subscribers' needs. Think of it as guiding a close friend through a decision-making process - you wouldn't start by pushing a sale, but rather by understanding their situation and gradually presenting solutions.

Start by consulting your customer journey map. This will inform how you craft each message, ensuring it aligns with where your subscribers are in their decision-making process. In the early stages, focus on building trust and showing that you understand their challenges. As they become more engaged, transition into educational content that positions your solution as a natural answer to their needs.

Your content should evolve through several key phases. Begin with awareness-building messages that demonstrate your expertise and understanding. Move into consideration-phase content, educating and illustrating solutions. When subscribers reach the decision stage, present clear value propositions backed by concrete evidence of success. After purchase, focus on ensuring their success and deepening the relationship.

To keep email sequences engaging, vary your content approach. Mix educational insights with real customer stories. Share industry expertise alongside practical how-to guidance. Include product information when relevant, always framing it in terms of subscriber benefit. Incorporate occasional promotional offers, ensuring they feel like natural next steps rather than aggressive sales tactics.

A strategic nurture sequence might flow like this:

1. **Initial Welcome:** *"Let's explore how we can help you succeed"*
2. **Challenge Recognition:** *"Breaking down your biggest obstacles"*
3. **Solution Discovery:** *"Proven strategies for success"*

4. **Methodology Introduction:** *"A fresh approach to solving [challenge]"*
5. **Confidence Building:** *"Why this approach works"*
6. **Clear Invitation:** *"Taking the next step together"*
7. **Timebound Opportunity:** *"Your pathway to success awaits"*

Remember, every email should provide genuine value, whether it's educational insights, practical tips, or exclusive offers. Your subscribers should look forward to hearing from you because each message helps them progress toward their goals.

Let's explore how to craft compelling subject lines and engaging content that will bring this sequence to life.

Crafting Compelling Subject Lines

The subject line represents perhaps the most critical element of the email nurture sequence. It serves as the initial point of contact with subscribers and determines whether carefully crafted content will ever be seen. Let us examine how to create subject lines that consistently engage your audience and drive meaningful open rates.

Think of your subject line as the first impression in a business meeting - it must be professional, engaging, and promise value in what follows. Every word must serve a purpose, as you have mere seconds to capture attention in an increasingly crowded inbox. Our goal is to craft subject lines that not only prompt opens, but also align with the valuable content, ensuring a consistent experience that builds trust with your audience.

Let's explore the key principles and strategies that transform your subject lines from simple headers into powerful tools for engagement.

Psychological Triggers: Pushing Those Brain Buttons

First things first, let's talk about what makes people tick (or in this case, click).

The effectiveness of subject lines relies heavily on their ability to tap into fundamental neuro-marketing principles that drive human behavior and decision-making. By understanding and thoughtfully implementing these psychological triggers, we create subject lines that naturally compel engagement while maintaining ethical marketing practices.

Curiosity

Curiosity serves as a powerful motivator in subject line creation. When we create a knowledge gap, readers naturally seek to resolve it. This principle proves particularly effective when aligned with your audience's professional interests or challenges. For example, a subject line that hints at unexplored industry insights or challenges common assumptions can capture attention by appealing to the natural desire for completion.

For example: *"The overlooked metric that's costing you clients"* or *"Why top performers are quietly changing their strategy."* These subject lines promise valuable information while leaving the specific revelation for the email content. *"Three unconventional lessons from our biggest failure"* combines curiosity with authenticity, suggesting valuable insights from real experience.

Scarcity and exclusivity

Scarcity and exclusivity tap into our inherent fear of missing opportunities. This doesn't merely mean adding *"limited time"* to every offer; rather, it involves creating genuine moments of exclusive value. Consider highlighting truly limited opportunities, special access to information, or time-sensitive insights that provide real competitive advantages.

Let's have a look at some examples for different scenarios:

Event and Capacity-Based: *"Executive roundtable: Five seats remaining for December"* resonates because physical limitations are inherently credible. Similarly, *"Q4 strategy workshop - Last three virtual spots"* creates natural scarcity through legitimate space constraints.

Early Access Opportunities: *"Preview our platform update before general release"* or *"Early access: Be among the first to explore our new research"* offer exclusive timing advantages without artificial pressure. These work well because they provide genuine priority access.

Resource-Limited Offerings: *"Schedule your year-end review - Eight consultation slots left"* or *"December strategy sessions: Four openings this quarter"* create scarcity based on realistic time and resource constraints that your audience understands.

Expertise-Based Exclusivity: *"Chief Analyst's private market insights - December edition"* or *"Invitation: Join our CMO's closed-door briefing"* create exclusivity through access to specific expertise or thought leadership.

Time-Sensitive but Natural: *"2024 forecast: Available to subscribers until Friday"* or *"Reserve your copy before public distribution"* create urgency tied to logical publication or distribution schedules.

The key is to base these subject lines on genuine limitations rather than artificial constraints. Your audience should understand why the limitation exists, making the exclusivity feel natural and valuable rather than manufactured.

Personal recognition

Personal recognition extends far beyond the simple inclusion of a recipient's name. Effective personalization demonstrates understanding of the recipient's industry, role, challenges, and recent interactions with your brand. This deeper level of personalization shows respect for your audience's specific context and creates immediate relevance.

Let's have a look at some examples for different scenarios:

Responding to Their Interests: *"The healthcare compliance update you asked about"* or *"More insights on scaling SaaS platforms"* is a natural follow-up to their expressed interests.

Professional Context: *"Your Q1 forecast tools - let's review together"* or *"Ready to walk through your team's metrics?"* acknowledges their role while offering genuine assistance.

Recent Interactions: *"Some answers to your questions from Tuesday"* or *"Quick update on what we discussed"* continues the conversation naturally, just as you would in person.

Company-Specific Context: *"Breaking down [Company Name]'s growth opportunities"* or *"Analysis of your market position for 2024"* shows you've done your homework without being overly familiar.

Progress Updates: *"First month's results are in"* or *"Your implementation roadmap - next steps"* ties to natural business milestones they care about.

Think of these as conversation starters rather than marketing messages. They should feel like something you'd naturally say to a colleague or business partner, maintaining professionalism while showing you understand their context and priorities.

Social validation

Social validation helps overcome initial skepticism by demonstrating that others have vetted or adopted your insights and solutions. This might involve sharing specific success metrics, highlighting notable adopters, or referencing industry benchmarks. The key lies in making these references specific and relevant to your audience's context.

Think of social validation as sharing relevant insights from industry peers - it should feel like a valuable insider perspective rather than obvious marketing.

Consider these subject line examples:

"What other CMOs are saying about the iOS update" sounds like you're sharing genuine peer insights rather than forcing social proof.

Similarly, *"How other startups are handling the funding slowdown"* offers valuable perspective from a relevant peer group.

"Interesting trends from your industry peers" or *"What we're hearing from other tech leaders"* gives the impression that you're

sharing helpful observations rather than pushing statistics. This approach works because it promises authentic insights rather than manufactured social proof.

"Other finance teams are approaching 2024 differently" suggests valuable peer insights while maintaining curiosity. *"What we learned from 100 successful implementations"* shares experience without feeling boastful.

Keep it conversational, as you would when sharing helpful observations with a colleague: *"Some interesting approaches from other companies in your space"* or *"Thought you'd find these peer insights helpful."*

The key is to make the subject lines read as though you're sharing valuable industry intelligence rather than bragging about numbers or name-dropping. It should feel like insider knowledge being passed along, not marketing statistics being pushed.

Remember to keep the focus on relevance to their situation: *"How similar companies are handling the new regulations"* or *"What your competitors might not be telling you"* connect peer insights directly to their context.

Urgency

Urgency, when used authentically, can motivate action without being manipulative. The most effective urgent subject lines tie to natural business cycles, market opportunities, and genuine deadlines rather than artificial constraints.

Think of it as akin to giving a helpful heads-up to a colleague about something they need to know:

"Regulatory changes coming next week - what to know" or *"Quick update before the new policy kicks in"* serves as a timely alert rather than manufactured pressure.

"Tomorrow's rate changes might affect your planning" or *"Sharing this before the market shifts"* creates urgency through relevant business context rather than artificial deadlines.

"Your window for Q1 planning is closing" or *"Last week to lock in current pricing"* works when there's a genuine business reason for the timeline.

Think timing-based rather than pressure-based: *"Getting this to you before your board meeting"* or *"Some insights for your upcoming strategy session"* connects urgency to actual schedules.

Market-driven urgency feels natural: *"The market's shifting - here's what we're seeing"* or *"Important changes happening in your sector"* suggests timely information rather than sales pressure.

Keep it helpful rather than pushy: *"Wanted you to see this before Thursday's announcement"* or *"A heads-up about next week's changes"* gives the impression that you're looking out for their interests.

Remember, the best urgency comes from real business context, not artificial pressure. It should come across as helping the reader to stay ahead of genuine deadlines or changes, avoiding creating false scarcity.

Beyond the more conventional psychological triggers, both humor and shock value serve as powerful tools in subject line creation, though they require careful implementation to maintain professionalism and brand integrity.

Humor

Humor, when properly executed, has the ability to differentiate emails in an otherwise serious inbox environment. It creates a moment of unexpected delight and humanizes your brand. However, humor must align with your brand voice and respect professional boundaries. Rather than attempting to be overtly funny, aim for clever wordplay or light-hearted observations related to your industry or audience's experiences.

For example: the subject line *"Your marketing strategy needs vitamin C: Content"* plays with familiar concepts while maintaining relevance. Remember that humor is highly subjective and should be tested carefully with the specific audience.

Here's how to keep it natural while still being engaging:

"Your data has trust issues" or *"Your analytics might be ghosting you"* adds a light touch to serious business topics, making them more approachable without undermining their importance.

"The meeting that should've been an email (is now an email)" shows self-awareness about business culture while delivering actual content. Similarly, *"Finally, a spreadsheet you'll actually want to open"* acknowledges common pain points with a smile.

"The ROI report your coffee needs to see first" or *"Your budget's secret admirer"* brings warmth to typically dry topics without being unprofessional.

Industry-specific humor works well: *"Your SEO strategy needs therapy"* or *"Your landing page is having an identity crisis"* speaks to shared experiences in a light-hearted way.

Keep it subtle and relevant: *"That awkward moment when your metrics tell the truth"*, or *"Your strategy called, it needs to talk"* maintains professionalism while adding personality.

Remember, the goal is to create a moment of recognition or

amusement, not to force a laugh. The humor should come from shared business experiences or challenges, coming across as authentic rather than forced.

Shock value

Shock value, when used strategically, has the potential to pattern-interrupt your audience's typical email scanning behavior. However, this approach requires a delicate balance. The goal is to surprise and intrigue, not to alienate or appear unprofessional. Consider challenging common industry assumptions or presenting unexpected statistics rather than using sensationalist tactics.

For example: *"Your customer feedback is lying to you"* creates intrigue while remaining professionally relevant.

The key to effective "shock value" in professional communication is to challenge assumptions or present unexpected perspectives without being sensational. Think thought-provoking rather than shocking:

"Everything you know about customer retention is outdated" or *"Your best customers might be your biggest problem"* challenges conventional wisdom while maintaining credibility.

"The uncomfortable truth about your conversion rates" or *"Why your most successful campaign actually failed"* presents a surprising

perspective that prompts reflection rather than shock.

"Your competitors are wrong (and so are you)" or *"The data says we've all been doing this backwards"* creates intrigue through respectful contradiction of established practices.

"Your strategy has a blind spot" or *"The metric you trust is lying to you"* suggests unexpected insights without becoming unprofessional.

Industry-specific challenges work well: *"Your AI isn't as intelligent as you think"* or *"Why your data dashboard is making things worse"* questions assumptions while promising valuable insights.

Remember, the goal is to present fresh perspectives that prompt people to think differently about familiar topics. Rather than feeling like clickbait, it should feel like a respected colleague offering an unexpected but well-reasoned viewpoint.

Keep it professional and backed by substance: *"The success metric that's actually holding you back"* or *"Your optimization strategy might be the problem"* promises insights that justify the initial surprise.

It is important to use both humor and shock value as occasional spice rather than a staple in subject line strategy. The effectiveness often lies in their unexpected nature, making them most powerful when interspersed among conventional approaches.

Key Implementation Guidelines:

- Maintain authenticity by ensuring perfect alignment between subject lines and email content
- Choose psychological triggers matching your audience's sophistication level
- Prioritize genuine valuable communication over clever wordplay
- Implement regular testing to understand trigger effectiveness

The goal isn't merely to generate opens but to begin meaningful conversations with your audience. Each subject line serves as a promise to your readers - a promise that must be fulfilled by the content that follows. When implementing these psychological triggers, always consider the long-term relationship you're building with your audience. A subject line that generates opens but disappoints with its content will ultimately harm your email marketing efforts.

A/B Testing Strategies: May the Best Subject Line Win

Even the most compelling subject line can be improved through systematic testing. Rather than relying on intuition alone, implementing a structured testing approach helps identify what truly resonates with your audience.

The process is straightforward but powerful. Begin by creating two variations of your subject line, maintaining the same core message while varying a single element. Send these versions to separate segments of your audience - typically 10-15% each of your total list. After gathering sufficient data to ensure statistical significance, analyze the performance metrics to determine which version generated better engagement. Following this, deploy the winning version to your remaining subscribers, ensuring optimal performance for the full campaign.

Key elements worth testing include the overall length of your subject line, the inclusion of personalization elements, and variations in tone. Consider testing professional versus conversational approaches, questions against statements, or the impact of including specific data points. While emojis have become common in email marketing, their effectiveness varies significantly by industry and audience - making them another essential element to test.

Keep your testing focused by varying one element at a time. For example, if you're testing subject line length, keep all other elements consistent between versions. This discipline ensures clear, actionable insights from each test.

Document your findings systematically. Each test contributes to a deeper understanding of your audience's preferences, gradually building a valuable playbook for future campaigns. This empirical approach takes the guesswork out of subject line creation, replacing assumptions with data-driven decisions.

Think of testing as an ongoing conversation with your audience, iteration bringing you closer to understanding what truly captures their attention and drives engagement.

Avoiding Spam Filters: Stay Out of Email Jail

Creating an engaging subject line serves little purpose if your email fails to reach your subscriber's inbox. Modern spam filters have become increasingly sophisticated, analyzing multiple elements to determine whether an email deserves inbox placement.

Several common practices trigger these filters. Using all capital letters in your subject line appears aggressive and unprofessional, while multiple exclamation points or excessive punctuation marks signal potential spam. Similarly, certain terms are red flags due to their historic association with spam campaigns - words like *"free,"* *"guarantee,"* and *"no obligation"* often trigger automatic filtering.

Take particular care with formatting conventions. Adding *"Re:"* or *"Fwd:"* to suggest an ongoing conversation when there isn't one violates trust and often triggers filters. Multiple dollar signs or symbols similarly raise suspicion. Most importantly, avoid making exaggerated claims or using clickbait tactics that promise more than your email delivers.

The key to consistent inbox placement lies in maintaining professional standards and honest communication. Modern email users - and the filters protecting them - respond best to straightforward, genuine subject lines that accurately reflect the email's content. This approach not only helps ensure delivery but also builds long-term trust with your audience.

Think of your subject line as a professional introduction - it should be polite, honest, and set appropriate expectations for the conversation to follow.

Subject Line Formulas: Your Secret Sauce

While creativity plays a vital role in crafting effective subject lines, certain structural frameworks consistently drive engagement. Understanding and adapting these proven approaches helps ensure subject lines maintain impact while feeling fresh and relevant.

The How-To

"How to [achieve desired result] in [timeframe]"

The *"How-To"* Framework addresses your audience's desire for practical solutions. Rather than the basic *"How to improve your metrics,"* consider more specific approaches like *"How to increase customer retention by 30% this quarter"* or *"How to streamline operations before peak season."* The key is combining concrete outcomes with realistic timeframes.

The List

"[Number] ways to [solve problem]"

List-based subject lines continue to perform well because they promise organized, digestible information. However, move beyond simple numbering. *"Five unexpected factors driving market change"* or *"Three critical shifts in consumer behavior"* offers more intrigue than basic listed items.

The Question

"Are you making these [industry] mistakes?"

Question-based subject lines work by prompting self-reflection. *"Is your growth strategy missing this crucial element?"* or *"What's really holding back your team's productivity?"* encourages recipients to seek answers within your email.

The Teaser

"You won't believe what happened when we [action]"

The teaser approach requires careful balance. Instead of clickbait, focus on genuine insight: *"What happened when we challenged conventional pricing models"* or *"The unexpected outcome of our latest market research."*

The Announcement

"Introducing: [New Product/Feature]"

Announcement frameworks should emphasize value rather than just features: *"Introducing: A new approach to supply chain resilience"* or *"Your strategy planning is about to get easier."*

The Personal

"[Name], I thought you'd like this"

Personalized subject lines extend beyond mere name insertion. *"Your industry's response to recent changes"* or *"Insights specific to your market challenges"* demonstrates understanding of recipient context.

The Curiosity Gap

"The surprising reason why [common belief] is wrong"

The curiosity gap framework succeeds by challenging established beliefs: *"Why traditional metrics are misleading your team"* or *"The counterintuitive truth about customer loyalty."*

The Countdown

"[Number] days left to [take action]"

Urgency-based frameworks should tie to genuine deadlines or opportunities: *"Key changes coming: Prepare your team by Friday"* or *"Last week to align with new regulations."*

Mix and match these formulas with your psychological triggers and you'll have an endless supply of subject line ideas!

The Preview Text: Your Subject Line's Sidekick

While subject lines command significant attention, the preview text plays an equally crucial role in driving engagement. This additional text snippet, visible in most email clients, provides valuable context and significantly influences open rates. Consider it an extension of the subject line - an opportunity to elaborate on your message's value before the recipient makes the decision to open.

Strategic use of preview text allows you to develop a complete narrative. When your subject line poses a question, the preview text can hint at the answer. When announcing new insights, it can preview the key takeaway. This complementary approach creates a compelling reason to engage with your full message.

Creating effective email openings requires balancing multiple elements - the science of testing and metrics, the art of engaging copy, and deep understanding of your audience's preferences and priorities. What resonates with a technical B2B audience may fall flat with creative professionals. Similarly, language that engages C-suite executives might not connect with operational managers.

Success in email marketing comes from continuous refinement of your approach. Test different combinations of subject lines and preview text, always measuring against your specific audience's response. Pay attention to which combinations drive not just opens, but meaningful engagement with your content.

The most effective approach aligns every element - from subject line through preview text to email content - to create a seamless, valuable experience for your recipients. This attention to detail helps establish the credibility and relevance that turns casual subscribers into engaged readers.

Let's move forward to explore how to craft email content that delivers on the promise of your carefully crafted openings.

Writing Engaging Email Content

Creating an effective email extends far beyond securing the initial open. Once you've captured your reader's attention with a compelling subject line, the content must deliver on its promise while maintaining engagement throughout. Let's explore how to craft messages that resonate and drive action.

Storytelling Techniques: Once Upon a Time in Email Land

Human beings are inherently drawn to stories - it's how we make sense of the world and connect with ideas. In email marketing, strategic storytelling transforms routine communications into compelling narratives that capture and hold attention.

Effective email narratives begin with a strong opening

immediately engaging the reader. Consider starting with a challenging moment that your audience will recognize: *"The quarterly results meeting was minutes away, and our data told an unexpected story."* This approach immediately creates connection through shared experience.

Building tension helps maintain interest throughout your message. Rather than presenting information linearly, create natural progression that pulls readers forward. For example, begin with a common industry challenge, explore its implications, then reveal unexpected insights or solutions.

Specific details and vivid language bring your message to life. Rather than stating *"Our solution improved efficiency,"* share a detailed account: *"Within three weeks, our client's processing time dropped from three days to three hours."* This concrete approach helps readers envision similar results in their context.

The most effective email stories maintain clear focus on your core message. Every anecdote, example, and case study need to reinforce the key points and lead naturally to the call to action. Think of your email as a brief, impactful business conversation - one that delivers value while respecting your reader's time.

Remember that your audience consists of busy professionals seeking valuable insights or solutions. While storytelling enhances engagement, ensure that the narrative serves your message rather than overshadowing it. Each story should illuminate the points while moving readers toward meaningful action.

Good stories in professional communication create connection, demonstrate understanding, and illustrate possibilities. They help readers see themselves in the narrative and envision positive outcomes from engaging with your message.

Personalization and Dynamic Content: Make It All About Them

Effective personalization goes far beyond inserting a subscriber's name into standardized content. It requires creating emails that genuinely reflect and respond to individual circumstances, preferences, and behaviors. Let's explore how to achieve meaningful personalization which enhances rather than diminishes communication.

Personal Recognition in Practice

While using a subscriber's name can add warmth to your communications, skillful personalization requires deeper consideration. Simple name insertion, particularly when overused, can feel mechanical rather than personal. Instead, focus on demonstrating genuine understanding of your recipient's context and needs.

Behavioral insight offers powerful opportunities for relevant personalization. When you reference specific interactions - *"Following up on your interest in our supply chain analysis"* or *"Based on your recent exploration of automation solutions"* - you demonstrate attentiveness to individual engagement patterns. This approach is more authentic than superficial personalization tactics.

Segmentation enables you to tailor content to specific audience characteristics. Consider factors such as:

- Industry context and challenges
- Professional role and responsibilities
- Organization size and complexity
- Geographic location and market conditions
- Past interactions and engagement patterns

Dynamic content adaptation takes personalization further by automatically adjusting email elements based on subscriber data. Ways to achieve this include showing different case studies to different industries and adjusting offers based on previous purchase patterns.

Important Technical Considerations

Always implement fallback options for personalization elements. Nothing undermines professionalism faster than visible personalization tokens in delivered emails. Ensure your system defaults to appropriate alternatives when specific data points are unavailable.

Remember that effective personalization serves your audience rather than showcasing technical capabilities. Every personalized element should enhance the value and relevance of communication for the recipient.

Neuro-Linguistic Programming (NLP) Principles: Jedi Mind Tricks for Emails

NLP might sound like scary brain science, but it's simply about communicating effectively. Understanding and applying principles from neuropsychology significantly enhances the impact of email content. This approach focuses on creating deeper connections through careful language selection and structure.

Engaging the Senses Through Language

Descriptive language which engages multiple senses creates vivid and memorable communications. Rather than presenting flat statements, incorporate rich descriptions, helping readers experience your message. For example, instead of describing a solution as *"efficient,"* detail how it transforms a chaotic workplace into a streamlined operation.

Aligning with Audience Perspective

Mirror your audience's language patterns and professional terminology to create natural resonance. When communications reflect the way your readers think and speak about their challenges, the message feels relevant and credible. Study industry conversations, common pain points, and preferred terminology to ensure your message fits naturally within the audience's professional context.

Progressive Communication Structure

Begin with shared understanding before introducing new concepts. Start with statements that align with your readers' known experiences or beliefs, then guide them naturally toward new insights or possibilities. This creates a comfortable path from familiar territory to fresh perspectives.

Positive Framing for Enhanced Impact

Focus on desired outcomes rather than problems to avoid. *"Achieve sustainable growth"* resonates more effectively than *"Stop losing market share."* This approach maintains optimism while addressing real challenges, helping readers envision positive change rather than dwelling on difficulties.

Language Choice and Assumption

Careful word selection can subtly influence how readers envision future outcomes. Phrases like "When you implement these changes" or "As you see these results" help readers imagine successful implementation, making positive outcomes feel more achievable.

Remember, these communication principles should enhance rather than manipulate your message, always serving to clarify and strengthen your core value proposition.

The Art of Persuasion: Creating Genuine Influence in Email Communications

Persuasive email marketing requires a delicate balance between encouraging action and maintaining trust. The most effective approach focuses on building credibility and demonstrating value rather than pushing for immediate responses.

Building Trust Through Social Validation

When others endorse your solutions or approach, it carries more weight than self-promotion. Share genuine customer experiences and concrete results rather than just numbers. For example, describing how specific organizations overcame common challenges using your solutions resonates powerfully compared to broad claims about customer satisfaction.

The Principle of Reciprocity and Value Exchange

Begin relationships by providing meaningful value before requesting action. Examples of this include sharing industry insights, offering practical solutions to common challenges, and providing useful tools and resources. When you consistently deliver value, subsequent requests feel like natural progression rather than an imposition.

Creating Legitimate Urgency

While scarcity and time-limited opportunities motivate action, they must be based on genuine limitations. Whether it's capacity constraints, implementation deadlines, or seasonal factors, ensure urgency stems from real business conditions rather than artificial pressure.

Establishing Authority Through Expertise

Share your expertise by providing unique insights and demonstrating a deep understanding of industry challenges. Rather than listing credentials, prove your authority through the value of your content and the clarity of your analysis. This approach builds credibility while remaining approachable.

The Power of Progressive Engagement

Build relationships through a series of smaller commitments which naturally lead to larger ones. When someone engages with your content or accepts an initial offer, they're more likely to consider more significant proposals. This graduated approach feels natural and respectful rather than pushy.

Remember that persuasion in professional communications works best when it arises from genuine value and mutual benefit rather than psychological manipulation.

Optimizing Email Structure for Modern Readers

In today's fast-paced business environment, professionals often review emails quickly while managing multiple priorities. Understanding and adapting to these reading patterns ensures your message receives proper attention and consideration.

Creating Visual Clarity

Structure your emails to facilitate quick comprehension. Keep paragraphs concise - typically two to three sentences - to maintain reader engagement. Generous use of white space between elements reduces cognitive load and makes the message inviting and accessible.

Strategic Content Organization

Break complex information into clear, logical sections with descriptive subheadings. This organization allows readers to quickly locate relevant information and understand the structure of the message. Where appropriate, use carefully crafted bullet points or numbered lists to present key information efficiently.

Emphasis and Hierarchy

Use formatting selectively to guide attention to crucial points. Bold text or italics effectively highlight essential information; however, overuse diminishes their impact. Consider your email's visual hierarchy - how different elements work together to guide readers through your message.

Remember that effective email structure serves both detailed readers and those who scan for key points. Your goal is to ensure that even a quick review conveys the essential message while inviting deeper engagement with the full content.

Think of your email's structure as a well-organized presentation - it should be clear, purposeful, and easy to follow, regardless of how deeply the reader chooses to engage.

Crafting Effective Calls-to-Action: Driving Meaningful Engagement

The effectiveness of emails ultimately depends on their ability to inspire action. A call-to-action (CTA) serves as the crucial bridge between reader engagement and tangible results. Let's explore how to create CTAs that drive a meaningful response.

Strategic CTA Development

Clarity and specificity prove essential in crafting effective CTAs. Rather than generic phrases like *"Click here"* or *"Learn more,"* use precise language communicating clear value: *"Access your industry report"* or *"Reserve your consultation time."* Specificity helps readers understand exactly what to expect from their action.

Visual Priority and Placement

Position your primary CTA where it naturally aligns with reader interest - typically after you've established value and before requiring excessive scrolling. While you may include secondary actions, ensure the main CTA stands out through clear design choices in color, size, or button styling.

Creating Motivation

When appropriate, incorporate genuine urgency or scarcity into the CTA. Rather than artificial pressure, focus on real limitations or timely opportunities: *"Secure your spot - Five consultation times remaining"* or *"Register before early-bird pricing ends."*

Maintaining Focus

While multiple CTAs seem tempting, concentrate on your primary objective. Additional options distract from the main goal. Consider the email's purpose, ensuring the CTA directly supports that outcome.

Remember, an effective CTA feels like a natural next step rather than an abrupt request. It must flow logically from your content and provide clear value to your reader.

The P.S. Is Your Secret Weapon

The postscript (P.S.) represents a powerful yet often underutilized element in email communications. Research consistently shows that readers pay particular attention to this final note, making it an excellent opportunity to reinforce key messages or provide additional value.

Leveraging the P.S. Effectively

A well-crafted postscript serves multiple strategic purposes. Use it to emphasize the main message, perhaps approaching it from a fresh angle or adding compelling context. It provides an ideal opportunity to reinforce urgency with specific deadlines or limited availability. Additionally, the P.S. offers a natural place for including valuable bonus information and sharing relevant personal insights that add depth to your message.

The postscript's effectiveness stems from its perceived informal nature - it feels like an afterthought but can be strategically planned to drive home key points or prompt action. Consider it a final opportunity to connect with readers who have skimmed your main content.

Creating Balance in Email Communications

Successful email content ultimately requires balancing multiple elements - informative value, engaging presentation, and persuasive call-to-actions - while maintaining professional credibility. The goal is to create communications which respect the readers' time while delivering meaningful value that keeps them engaged with future messages.

Now that the content is in place, in the next section, we'll talk about making your emails look as good as they read. Get ready to flex those design muscles!

Email Design Principles

The visual presentation of email content plays a crucial role in its effectiveness. While compelling content forms the foundation of a message, thoughtful design ensures communication is both accessible and engaging across all devices and platforms.

Mobile-First Design Strategy

With the majority of professionals accessing emails through mobile devices, optimizing emails for mobile viewing is essential. This shift in user behavior demands a refined approach to email design that both prioritizes mobile accessibility and maintains desktop functionality. Here are some key design considerations:

Structure and Layout

A single-column design provides optimal readability across devices. This streamlined approach ensures content flows naturally on smaller screens while maintaining the impact on larger displays. Consider limiting email width to 600 pixels which ensures proper scaling across platforms.

Interactive Elements

CTA buttons and interactive elements must accommodate touch-based interaction. Design these elements with sufficient size and spacing to ensure easy activation on mobile devices. This typically means creating buttons at least 44 pixels in height to accommodate comfortable thumb interaction.

Typography and Readability

Font selection and sizing significantly impacts readability. Body text should be at least 14 pixels, with headlines at 22 pixels or larger to ensure comfortable reading on mobile screens. Choose clear, web-safe fonts that maintain legibility across devices.

Testing Protocol

Implement comprehensive testing across multiple devices and email clients to ensure consistent presentation. This includes reviewing the design on various screen sizes, operating systems, and email applications to verify proper rendering and functionality.

Remember that effective mobile design typically translates well to desktop viewing, making a mobile-first approach particularly valuable. This strategy ensures optimal user experience regardless of how recipients access your communications.

Visual Hierarchy: Guide Their Eyes Like A Pro

The organization and presentation of visual elements significantly influence how readers process and retain your message. Understanding and implementing proper visual hierarchy ensures key points receive appropriate attention while maintaining overall readability.

Strategic Element Placement

Size variation serves as a natural indicator of importance in visual communications. Larger elements naturally draw attention, making this technique particularly effective for headlines and key messages. However, use size differentials judiciously to maintain professional appearance and prevent visual overwhelm.

Contrast and Readability

Ensuring strong contrast between text and background colors is key to enhancing readability and minimizing eye strain. The classic combination of dark text on a light background usually offers the best readability, but it's important to verify that your chosen colors provide sufficient contrast for comfortable reading on various devices and in different lighting environments.

Moreover, be mindful of colorblind (for those that do not know, I am colorblind) readers by avoiding potentially problematic color pairings, such as red and green, and making sure all text is clearly distinguishable regardless of color perception. By doing so, you ensure your emails are accessible to a wider audience, including those with color vision deficiencies.

Utilizing Negative Space

Thoughtful use of white space helps prevent visual clutter and guides attention to key elements. Rather than filling every available area, allow content to breathe through strategic spacing. This approach not only improves readability, but also creates a sophisticated, professional appearance.

Natural Reading Patterns

Research shows that readers typically scan digital content in an

F-shaped pattern, beginning at the top left. Position critical information along this natural reading path to ensure it receives proper attention. This might mean placing key messages and CTA where they naturally intersect with this scanning pattern.

Visual Support Elements

When incorporating images or graphics, ensure they enhance rather than compete with the message. Each visual element should serve a specific purpose in supporting communication objectives. Consider how graphics and text work together to convey your message effectively.

The ultimate goal is to create a clear, intuitive reading experience that guides your audience through your content while emphasizing key messages. Focus on functionality and clarity rather than purely aesthetic considerations.

Color Psychology: Painting Emotions with Your Palette

Color choice plays a fundamental role in shaping how recipients perceive and respond to your email communications. Understanding the psychological impact of different colors enables you to create more effective, emotionally resonant messages that align with your communication objectives.

Color Impact and Meaning

Each color carries specific associations and influences reader perception in distinct ways. Blue tones typically convey professionalism and reliability, making them particularly effective for business communications and trust-building messages. Green suggests growth and stability, often resonating well in financial or development-focused content.

Red, while powerful for creating emphasis or urgency, requires careful application to avoid overwhelming readers. Yellow introduces optimism and energy to the design, and purple often signals sophistication or innovation. Orange strikes a balance between professionalism and approachability, positioning it as effective for friendly, confident communications.

Implementation Strategy

Maintain visual coherence by limiting your color palette to two or three primary colors. This constraint creates a clean, professional appearance while preventing visual confusion. Ensure your chosen colors align with your brand guidelines and industry expectations while supporting your message's intended tone.

Consider your audience's cultural and professional context when selecting colors. Different industries and cultures may interpret colors differently; therefore, it is essential to understand your specific audience's expectations and associations.

Remember that effective color usage subtly enhances the message rather than dominating it. The goal is to create a harmonious design that supports communication objectives and maintains professional credibility.

Typography: Font-astic Ways to Capture Attention

Typography forms a crucial element of email design, significantly impacting readability and brand perception. Strategic font selection and implementation ensure your message is not only received but also properly understood and remembered.

Font Selection Principles

Limit your typography selection to two or three complementary fonts to maintain visual coherence. Consider designating specific fonts for different content elements: one for headlines to capture attention, another for body text to ensure readability, and potentially a third for specific accent elements or CTA.

Digital Readability Considerations

Sans-serif fonts provide superior readability in digital formats, as their clean lines render clearly across different screen sizes and resolutions. This becomes particularly important when considering the variety of devices and email clients your recipients might use.

Typography Scale and Spacing

Font size significantly impacts readability and engagement. Headlines ought to command attention while body text maintains comfortable reading size across devices. Proper line spacing, ideally set at 1.5 times the font size, prevents visual crowding and enhances readability. This spacing allows readers to move easily between lines without losing their place or experiencing eye strain.

Text Alignment Strategy

Left alignment provides the most natural reading experience for most western audiences, creating a consistent starting point for each line. Reserve center alignment for short, impactful elements such as headlines or CTA where symmetry enhances visual appeal without compromising readability.

Remember that effective typography supports the message rather than drawing attention to itself. Your goal is to create a seamless reading experience which allows the content to shine while maintaining professional presentation.

Images and Graphics: Worth a Thousand Words (If You Use Them Right)

The thoughtful incorporation of visual elements significantly enhances email engagement and comprehension. However, successful implementation requires careful balance between visual impact and technical considerations to ensure optimal delivery and accessibility.

Technical Optimization

Image file size plays a crucial role in email performance. Large files can impede loading times and potentially trigger spam filters, compromising delivery success. Optimize all visual elements for email delivery while maintaining quality, ensuring quick loading across various connection speeds and devices.

Accessibility Considerations

Implement descriptive alternative text for all images to maintain message clarity when images fail to load or when recipients use screen readers. This practice not only supports accessibility but also ensures your message remains effective even when visual elements are disabled or unavailable.

Strategic Visual Selection

Human faces typically generate strong engagement, creating immediate emotional connection with your content. When appropriate, incorporate professional photography of people to enhance message resonance and build trust.

Information Visualization

Complex information often benefits from visual representation through carefully designed infographics. Focus on clarity and simplicity, ensuring that visual elements enhance rather than complicate understanding. Break down complex concepts into digestible visual components supporting the written message.

Dynamic Elements

While animated GIFs add engaging movement to your emails, use them judiciously. Consider both file size implications and potential distraction from the core message. When implementing animation, ensure it serves a specific purpose in supporting communication objectives.

Remember that visual elements must enhance your message rather than overshadow it. Each image or graphic should serve a clear purpose in advancing your communication goals while maintaining professional presentation standards.

The Power of Plain Text: When Simple Emails Make Strategic Sense

While carefully designed HTML emails serve many purposes, there are times when a simple, plain-text approach proves more effective. Understanding when and how to utilize standard email formats enhances personal connection and improves engagement in specific situations.

Strategic Application

Plain-text or minimally formatted emails often perform exceptionally well for personal communications, senior executive outreach, or relationship-building sequences. Their simplicity suggests individual attention rather than mass marketing, creating an intimate connection with recipients.

Formatting Best Practices

Even within the constraints of standard email clients, thoughtful formatting enhances readability:

- Keep paragraphs brief and focused, typically two to three lines
- Use simple bullet points (standard keyboard characters) for lists
- Create visual breaks between sections with strategic line spacing

- Incorporate subtle emphasis through selective use of bolding or italics
- Maintain a clean, consistent signature format

Link Presentation

When including links, consider placing them on separate lines or clearly offsetting them within the text. While you can't create designed buttons, careful placement and clear contextual descriptions enable links to stand out.

Personal Touch Elements

Standard email formats excel at conveying authenticity. Consider including elements reinforcing personal connection:

- Reference specific details about previous interactions
- Use a direct, conversational tone
- Include personal signoffs when appropriate
- Add relevant context about why you're reaching out

Technical Considerations

Plain-text emails offer these advantages:

- Consistent rendering across all email clients
- Improved deliverability rates
- Faster loading times
- Better compatibility with mobile devices

- Higher engagement in certain professional contexts

Remember that sometimes the most effective approach is also the simplest. A well-crafted plain-text email can achieve better results than an elaborately designed alternative, particularly when personal connection is your primary objective.

Maintaining Visual Consistency in Email Communications

Brand consistency across your email communications builds recognition and reinforces professional credibility. When recipients instantly recognize your emails through consistent design elements, the brand association is strengthened, and trust is built through familiarity.

Establishing Design Standards

Develop a core email template which serves as the foundation for all communications. This master template should reflect your brand's visual identity while maintaining flexibility for different types of content. Think of it as creating a signature look that recipients immediately associate with your organization.

Brand Alignment

Ensure email design elements mirror your broader brand presence. Email communications should feel like a natural extension of your website and other marketing materials. This includes maintaining consistency in:

- Color schemes and usage patterns
- Typography selections and hierarchies
- Visual style and imagery approach
- Tone and presentation of information

Header Design and Recognition

Create a distinctive yet professional header that appears consistently across all emails. This typically includes your logo and key brand elements, establishing immediate visual recognition when recipients open your messages.

Structural Elements

Maintain consistency in how you present recurring elements throughout emails:

- Call-to-action styling and placement
- Section header formatting
- Content block organization

- Footer information and layout

Remember that consistency in email design isn't about limiting creativity but rather creating a reliable framework supporting effective communication while building brand recognition.

Accessibility: Design for Everyone

Email accessibility transcends basic design preferences to ensure communications reach and engage every member of your audience effectively. Thoughtful implementation of accessibility principles enhances user experience for all recipients, not just those with specific needs.

Visual Design Considerations

Contrast plays a fundamental role in readability. Strong contrast between text and background colors ensures comfortable reading across various devices and lighting conditions. However, accessibility extends beyond contrast alone - incorporate multiple visual and textual cues to convey important information, rather than relying solely on color differentiation.

Navigation and Interaction

Clear link identification enables users to navigate content

effectively. Underlined text and distinct colors for hyperlinks provide clear visual cues for clickable elements. More importantly, use descriptive link text clearly indicating the destination or action, enabling both visual readers and those using screen readers to understand the purpose of each link.

Content Structure and Organization

Implement a clear hierarchical structure using proper heading levels (H1, H2, etc.) to organize content logically. This approach not only helps screen readers interpret your content correctly but also creates natural visual organization that benefits readers.

Technical Implementation

Consider these essential elements for accessible email design:

- Semantic HTML for proper content structure
- Alt text for all meaningful images
- Logical reading order in the HTML
- Adequate text size and line spacing
- Mobile-friendly responsive design

Remember that accessible design creates better experiences for everyone. Focus on creating clear, well-structured communications that recipients can easily navigate and understand, regardless of how they access your content.

Moving forward, we'll explore how to create compelling CTAs that build upon these foundational design principles to drive engagement and response.

Effective Calls-to-Action

The CTA turns reader interest into real results. While compelling content draws readers in, effective CTAs provide clear direction for next steps, guiding recipients toward meaningful action.

Strategic Positioning

The placement of a CTA significantly influences its effectiveness. Position the primary CTA where it naturally aligns with reader interest and understanding - typically after you've established value and before requiring extensive scrolling. This approach ensures visibility while maintaining logical progression from content to action.

Building to Action

Structure email content to create natural momentum toward the CTA. Present your value proposition and supporting evidence in a way that makes the CTA feel like a logical next step rather than an abrupt request. The most effective CTAs emerge naturally from well-crafted content which anticipates and addresses the needs of the reader.

Visual Prominence

In longer communications, consider strategic repetition of your CTA, maintaining focus on a primary objective while providing multiple opportunities for engagement. However, ensure that secondary CTAs support rather than compete with your main goal. The primary CTA ought to maintain clear visual prominence through strategic design elements.

Natural Eye Movement

Consider natural reading patterns when positioning the CTA. As mentioned earlier, the majority of readers scan digital content in an F-shaped pattern, making the left side and upper portion of your email particularly valuable real estate for key elements. Position your CTA where it intersects naturally with this scanning pattern.

Testing Effectiveness

Employ the "squint test" to evaluate your CTA's visual prominence - when viewing the email with slightly blurred vision, the CTA should remain clearly distinguishable from surrounding content. This simple test helps ensure your CTA maintains sufficient visual priority to capture attention effectively.

Remember that effective CTAs serve as natural bridges between reader interest and meaningful engagement. Focus on creating clear, compelling CTAs aligned with both user needs and business objectives.

Design: Make It Pop!

The visual presentation of your CTA plays a crucial role in its effectiveness. While the message itself drives response, thoughtful design ensures your CTA receives appropriate attention and enables easy interaction across all devices.

Button Design Principles

Research consistently demonstrates that button-style CTAs generate higher engagement rates than simple text links. The three-dimensional appearance of buttons naturally signals interactivity, enabling readers to instantly recognize clickable elements. However, effectiveness lies in balanced design - buttons should command attention without appearing aggressive or misaligned with your overall aesthetic.

Mobile Optimization

It is important for contemporary email design to prioritize mobile usability. Ensure buttons maintain sufficient size and spacing to accommodate touch interaction - typically a minimum of 44 pixels in height with adequate padding. This prevents frustration on mobile devices while maintaining professional appearance on desktop displays.

Color and Contrast

Select colors that create clear visual distinction between your CTA and surrounding elements while maintaining brand consistency. Effective contrast draws attention naturally without requiring dramatic design elements. Consider how your chosen colors perform across different devices and lighting conditions.

Spatial Considerations

Strategic use of white space around your CTA enhances visual impact and improves usability. Provide sufficient padding to prevent accidental clicks while creating a clear visual break that draws attention to the CTA. This breathing room helps prevent visual competition with surrounding content.

Remember that effective CTA design supports rather than overshadows your message. Focus on creating clear, accessible interaction points guiding recipients toward desired actions while maintaining professional presentation standards.

Crafting Compelling CTA Language

The specific language used in your CTA fundamentally influences response rates. Effective CTA copy combines clarity, motivation, and specificity to prompt immediate action while maintaining professional credibility.

Active Language Selection

Begin your CTA with strong, action-oriented verbs clearly indicating the next step. Words such as *"Download," "Reserve," "Access,"* and *"Schedule"* immediately signal what action follows. This directness helps recipients understand exactly what happens when they engage with your CTA.

Specificity in Messaging

Move beyond generic phrases to communicate clear value.

Rather than *"Learn More,"* specify what knowledge or benefit awaits: *"Access Industry Research"* or *"View Market Analysis."* This precision helps recipients evaluate and commit to the proposed action.

Creating Measured Urgency

Incorporate time sensitivity when appropriate, while at the same time maintaining professionalism. Phrases such as *"Secure Early Access"* or *"Reserve Your Spot"* create natural urgency without appearing aggressive. This approach motivates action while preserving trust.

Effective Message Formulas

Several proven structures consistently drive engagement:

- *"Access Your [Specific Benefit]"*
- *"Begin Your [Relevant Process]"*
- *"Join [Specific Group/Program]"*
- *"Secure Your [Valuable Resource]"*

Keep messaging concise and focused, typically between two and five words. Each word should contribute meaningfully to understanding or motivation.

Remember that effective CTA language balances motivation with authenticity. Focus on clearly communicating value while maintaining professional tone and credibility.

Creating Urgency and Scarcity: The Fear of Missing Out (FOMO) Factor

The strategic use of urgency and scarcity powerfully drives action when it stems from authentic limitations. The key lies in communicating real deadlines and limitations while maintaining professional credibility.

Time-Sensitive Opportunities

When legitimate time constraints exist - such as early registration periods, seasonal opportunities, or limited enrollment windows - communicate these clearly to your audience. For instance, if you're hosting a workshop with limited capacity, let recipients know: *"Q1 Strategy Workshop: Registration closes December 15"* or *"Early pricing available through Friday."* The urgency flows naturally from real business conditions rather than artificial pressure.

Limited Availability

Occasionally scarcity arises from genuine resource constraints. Whether you're offering one-on-one consultations, workshop seats, or exclusive program access, be transparent about limitations. *"Six consultation slots available for December"* feels more authentic than vague claims of limited availability.

Supporting Visual Elements

While countdown timers and availability indicators effectively remind recipients of approaching deadlines, use them judiciously and only when representing actual constraints. These elements are meant to support rather than create urgency.

Exclusive Access

When providing special opportunities to specific audience segments, frame this exclusivity in terms of value rather than pressure. *"Priority access for existing clients"* or *"Exclusive to quarterly report subscribers"* acknowledges the special nature of the offer while maintaining professional tone.

The Trust Factor

Above all, maintain authenticity in your communications. Every deadline or limitation needs to reflect genuine business conditions. Recipients quickly recognize artificial scarcity, which damages the effort of long-term relationship building. Focus on communicating real value and legitimate constraints rather than manufacturing urgency.

Remember, the most effective urgency comes from genuine opportunities with natural limitations. Your role is to inform rather than pressure, ensuring recipients make timely decisions about valuable opportunities.

Reducing Friction: Make It Easy to Say Yes

Understanding and addressing potential hesitation points significantly improves response rates to CTAs. Success often lies in making the next step feel manageable and low risk for your recipients.

Anticipating Concerns

Consider potential common objections or hesitations your audience may have, addressing these directly in your CTA or supporting text. For instance, *"Begin your trial - No credit card needed"* immediately alleviates a common concern about unexpected charges. Similarly, *"Preview the platform - No installation required"* removes technical anxiety before it can prevent action.

Setting Clear Expectations

Help recipients understand exactly what happens when they

respond. Phrases like *"Schedule a brief demo - 20 minutes"* or *"Download instant access guide"* clearly communicate the time investment and immediate outcome. This transparency enables recipients to commit to action with confidence.

Risk Reduction

When appropriate, incorporate assurances that reduce perceived risk. *"Explore with 30-day money-back guarantee"* or *"Start with complimentary consultation" aids* in overcoming initial hesitation by minimizing potential downsides.

Graduated Commitment Levels

Match your CTA to your recipient's likely stage in the decision process. Early-stage prospects respond better to *"View capabilities guide"* rather than *"Purchase now."* This alignment with their readiness level builds trust while maintaining engagement.

Remember that reducing friction means anticipating and addressing concerns before they become barriers to action. Focus on creating clear, low-risk paths to engagement aligning with your recipients' comfort levels.

Personalization: Make It All About Them

Personalization transforms standard CTAs into relevant, engaging prompts speaking directly to each recipient's situation. When done thoughtfully, this targeted approach significantly improves response rates while building stronger professional relationships.

Understanding Your Audience

Start with what you know about each recipient. Their industry role, previous interactions, and specific challenges all inform how you frame your CTA. For instance, if you're sharing industry research, a CFO might respond better to *"Review financial implications"* while a COO might prefer *"Explore operational impacts."*

Building on Past Engagement

Let previous interactions guide your approach. When someone has shown interest in specific topics or solutions, acknowledge this continuity. *"Based on your interest in automation, you'll find value in our latest implementation guide"* creates a natural progression in the conversation.

Tailoring by Segment

Different audience segments require distinct approaches.

Technical teams may appreciate detailed, specification-focused CTAs, while business leaders might respond better to strategic, outcome-focused language. Consider adjusting both the offer and its presentation based on who you're addressing.

Smart Content Adaptation

Use available data wisely to adjust offers and language. If you know a recipient's industry challenges or recent purchases, reference these specifically. *"See how other manufacturing leaders are solving this"* feels more relevant than a generic *"Learn more"* approach.

Remember, the goal isn't to prove how much you know about your recipient, but rather to make their next step feel natural and valuable. Focus on creating CTAs that demonstrate understanding while maintaining professional rapport.

Now that you've got your CTAs sorted, your emails are primed for action! In the next section, we'll dive into the fascinating world of behavioral psychology and how you can use it to make emails even more effective. Get ready to become an email mind reader (sort of)!

Neuro-Marketing and Cognitive Bias in Emails

Understanding how the brain processes information and makes decisions provides powerful insights for email marketing. By leveraging established patterns of human cognition and decision-making, we are able to craft compelling communications, seamlessly aligning with the recipients' perspectives and behaviors.

The field of neuro-marketing reveals how cognitive processes influence response to marketing communications. This isn't about manipulation - it's about understanding the neural pathways and mental shortcuts which shape how people engage with information. By understanding these patterns, we have the ability to create messages which resonate effectively with natural thought processes.

Cognitive biases, those mental shortcuts our brains use to process information and make decisions, play a crucial role in how recipients interact with emails. These aren't flaws to exploit, but rather natural tendencies to understand and accommodate in communication strategies. By recognizing these patterns, we are able to structure our messages to work with, rather than against, natural cognitive processes.

This approach focuses on aligning email communications with established patterns of human thought and decision-making. Understanding these fundamental aspects of brain function and cognitive processing helps create messages that are intuitive and relevant to recipients while achieving our communication objectives.

Let's explore how understanding these neurological and cognitive principles enhance the effectiveness of email marketing while maintaining ethical practices and building stronger connections with your audience.

The Reciprocity Principle: Give and You Shall Receive

Human beings naturally feel inclined to reciprocate when they receive value. This fundamental aspect of human behavior enhances email marketing effectiveness when approached thoughtfully and authentically.

Creating Genuine Value Exchange

Begin relationships by offering meaningful value without immediate expectation of return. Examples of this are providing comprehensive industry research, practical tools for common challenges, and exclusive insights to help recipients address pressing business needs. The key lies in ensuring these offerings deliver real value rather than merely setting up a transaction.

Unexpected Value Addition

Periodically surprise your audience with additional resources or benefits. You could share an extra research report with your regular industry analysis or provide complementary tools with the standard content. These unexpected additions foster stronger positive associations than standard, anticipated benefits.

Knowledge Sharing

Share your expertise generously through detailed insights, practical frameworks, and actionable recommendations. When recipients benefit from your knowledge, they become receptive to future communications and offerings.

For example, you might send a message like: *"Based on recent industry changes, we've developed a comprehensive analysis of emerging opportunities. Access the complete report below. We hope this helps inform your strategic planning."*

Remember that reciprocity works best when the initial value offered is genuine and substantial. Focus initially on providing actual benefit to your recipients; positive responses will develop naturally from that foundation.

The goal is to build relationships based on mutual value rather than obligation. When recipients consistently receive meaningful benefits from your communications, they're more likely to engage deeply with future messages and consider your offerings.

Social Proof: Everybody's Doing It

Decision-making is often influenced by the actions and experiences of others, particularly in professional contexts. Understanding and thoughtfully incorporating social validation significantly enhances the impact of email communications.

Demonstrating Market Adoption

Share specific, verifiable evidence of how others have benefited from your solutions and insights. Rather than broad claims, provide detailed examples: *"327 financial institutions implemented this approach in Q3, averaging 23% efficiency improvement."* This builds credibility while offering concrete reference points for decision-making.

Industry Leadership Validation

Reference meaningful recognition from respected sources within your industry. Whether through analyst reports, industry awards, or media coverage, third-party validation adds credibility to your message. Rather than general accolades, focus on recognition that matters to your specific audience.

Peer Experience Sharing

Include relevant case studies and success stories resonating with your audience's specific challenges. For instance, *"See how three Fortune 500 manufacturers resolved similar supply chain challenges"* speaks directly to others facing similar situations.

Quantifiable Impact

When sharing statistics, use precise numbers that reflect actual results. *"1,847 organizations achieved compliance using this framework"* carries more weight than rounded numbers that might appear estimated. This precision suggests careful tracking and genuine results.

Remember that social proof is most effective when relevant to your specific audience and challenges they face. Focus on sharing validation helping recipients to understand how others in similar situations have succeeded, rather than simply broadcasting popularity.

The goal is to help recipients make informed decisions by understanding how others have successfully addressed similar challenges or opportunities.

Loss Aversion:

The brain processes potential losses more intensely than equivalent gains. This cognitive tendency influences professional decision-making, particularly when evaluating opportunities and allocating resources. Understanding this helps create compelling communications which respect professional sensibilities while driving timely action.

Time-Sensitive Opportunities

When genuine deadlines and time limitations exist, communicate them clearly and professionally. For instance, *"Early registration pricing available through December 15"* or *"Q1 implementation slots filling quickly"* creates natural urgency based on business constraints.

Access-Based Motivation

When offering exclusive or limited access to valuable resources, communicate the unique nature of the opportunity. *"Reserved for current clients: Advanced feature preview"* or *"Limited seating: Executive roundtable with industry leaders"* helps recipients understand what they might miss by delaying action.

Resource Limitations

When genuine scarcity exists - whether in consultation availability, program slots, or implementation windows - communicate these constraints transparently. *"Three December strategy sessions remaining"* provides clear, actionable information regarding limited availability.

Opportunity Costs

Enable recipients to understand the potential impact of delayed action without resorting to pressure tactics. *"Teams implementing by Q1 typically see full benefits by Q3"* focuses on positive outcomes while highlighting the value of timely action.

Remember that professional audiences respond best to authentic limitations communicated transparently. Focus on helping recipients make informed decisions about genuine opportunities rather than creating artificial pressure.

The goal is to ensure recipients have the information they need to evaluate opportunities effectively and take timely action when appropriate.

The Zeigarnik Effect: The Power of Unfinished Business

Understanding and leveraging the brain's natural inclination to seek closure enhances email engagement. This cognitive tendency to remember and pursue unfinished tasks offers valuable opportunities for structuring email communications, maintaining ongoing interest.

Strategic Content Sequencing

Organize complex information into logical sequences that build upon each other. For instance, *"Strategic Planning Series: Phase 1 - Market Analysis"* leads recipients to anticipate and engage with subsequent communications. This approach helps maintain engagement while ensuring comprehensive understanding of complex topics.

Anticipation Building

Create natural progression in your communication flow. Rather than delivering all information at once, strategically preview upcoming insights: *"Next week: Key findings from our industry analysis"* or *"Coming Thursday: Critical factors driving market shifts."* This approach maintains engagement while ensuring each piece of information receives proper attention.

Progress Visualization

When appropriate, help recipients track their advancement through important processes or learning sequences. Whether implementing new systems, completing training, or working through strategic planning, visual progress indicators maintain momentum and engagement.

Implementation Frameworks

Structure complex implementations and learning sequences into clear stages. For instance, *"Platform Optimization: Step 2 of 5 - Advanced Features"* helps recipients understand their progress while maintaining focus on completion.

Remember that this approach works best when each component delivers genuine value while building toward meaningful conclusions. Focus on creating sequences that enhance understanding and implementation rather than artificially extending engagement.

The goal is to maintain natural engagement through valuable content progression rather than manufactured suspense.

The Framing Effect: It's All About Perspective

How we present information significantly influences how it's received and processed. Understanding this cognitive principle enables us to communicate effectively while maintaining professional credibility.

Positive Outcome Focus

Frame solutions and opportunities in terms of achievable gains rather than avoided losses. *"Increase operational efficiency by 50%"* resonates more effectively than *"Reduce operational waste."* Similarly, *"Achieve target metrics consistently"* creates more positive engagement than "Stop missing performance goals."

Value Perspective

Present investment decisions in contexts that align with their true value. For instance, *"Investment per team member: $8 daily"* often provides more meaningful context than *"Annual enterprise license: $25,000."* Using this approach allows recipients to better evaluate value relative to impact.

Opportunity Emphasis

Structure messages to highlight positive engagement rather than negative consequences. *"Join industry leaders implementing these strategies"* creates more positive associations than *"Don't fall behind industry standards."* Focus on inclusion and advancement rather than exclusion or loss.

Implementation Framing

When discussing change or new initiatives, emphasize improvement and enhancement rather than correction or replacement. *"Optimize your current processes"* typically receives better reception than *"Fix your broken system."*

Remember that effective framing maintains complete honesty while helping recipients understand true value and opportunity. Focus on presenting accurate information in ways that facilitate clear understanding and decision-making.

The goal is to help recipients evaluate opportunities and information from the most relevant and meaningful perspective while maintaining complete transparency.

The Anchoring Effect: Setting the Right Reference Point

The anchoring effect happens when the first piece of information we see or hear affects how we think about later information. For example, if you first hear that a shirt costs $100, you might think $50 is a great deal for the same shirt—even if $50 is still expensive. That first price ($100) becomes an "anchor" that influences how you judge the value of other prices. It demonstrates how our minds tend to rely too much on the first number or detail we receive when making decisions.

Understanding this cognitive principle helps structure communications that enable clearer value assessment while maintaining professional integrity.

Establishing Value Context

When presenting solutions or opportunities, provide meaningful reference points that help recipients evaluate true value. For instance, highlight comprehensive enterprise solutions before introducing targeted options, allowing recipients to understand the full spectrum of possibilities.

Investment Comparisons

Present investment decisions within relevant market contexts.

Rather than focusing solely on cost, demonstrate value through meaningful comparisons: *"Enterprise capabilities at mid-market investment levels"* or *"Full-suite functionality at 40% below typical industry investment."*

Solution Positioning

Structure offerings to help recipients understand relative value. Begin with comprehensive solutions showcasing full capabilities, then present focused options that may better align with specific needs or constraints. This approach helps recipients make informed decisions based on their unique requirements.

Market Context

When appropriate, provide industry benchmarks or standard investment levels, enabling recipients to evaluate opportunities effectively. *"Traditional implementation costs typically exceed $250,000; our streamlined approach delivers complete functionality at $145,000"* offers valuable context for decision-making.

Remember that reference points should enhance understanding rather than manipulate perception. Focus on providing genuine, helpful context which enables informed decision-making while maintaining complete transparency.

The goal is to help recipients better understand true value and make well-informed decisions based on complete, contextual information.

The Paradox of Choice: Less Can Be More

While options provide flexibility, excessive choice can impede decision-making. Understanding this cognitive principle helps create communications that facilitate clear, confident decisions while maintaining professional sophistication.

Strategic Option Presentation

Present choices in manageable sets that facilitate decisive action. Rather than overwhelming recipients with numerous alternatives, offer carefully curated options addressing distinct needs or scenarios. For instance, present three clear solution tiers: standard, advanced, and enterprise, each serving specific organizational requirements.

Clear Recommendations

Guide decision-making by highlighting solutions best serving common use cases. *"Most organizations with your profile achieve optimal results with our advanced package"* provides helpful direction while respecting recipient autonomy.

Progressive Information Delivery

Structure complex offerings in digestible layers. Begin with core solutions that address fundamental needs. Following this, as recipients demonstrate interest or requirement, introduce advanced capabilities or customization options. This approach prevents initial overwhelm while maintaining access to comprehensive options.

Focused Decision Paths

Create clear decision frameworks assisting recipients to navigate choices effectively. *"Based on your industry and scale, consider these two implementation approaches"* narrows focus to relevant options while ensuring appropriate solution fit.

Remember that simplifying choice architecture ought to enhance rather than limit recipient options. Focus on creating clear decision paths that lead to optimal outcomes while maintaining flexibility for unique requirements.

The goal is to facilitate confident, well-informed decisions by presenting options in ways that clarify rather than complicate the selection process.

The Commitment and Consistency Principle: Small Yeses Lead to Big Yeses

According to the Commitment and Consistency Principle, getting someone to agree to small things makes it easier for them to say yes to bigger things later. In the context of professional relationships, starting with small commitments helps build trust and credibility over time, leading to strong, long-lasting partnerships. This approach fosters effective engagement as people feel consistent with their earlier choices.

Building Trust Through Progressive Steps

Begin relationships with low-barrier value exchanges that demonstrate expertise and reliability. Offering valuable insights or resources - such as industry analysis reports or strategic frameworks - establishes credibility while allowing recipients to engage comfortably at their own pace.

Natural Relationship Development

Structure engagement opportunities that build logically upon previous interactions. When someone has found value in your thought leadership content, they're more likely to engage with specialized insights or targeted solutions. *"Following your interest in our supply chain analysis, we've prepared detailed implementation frameworks"* creates natural progression.

Engagement Recognition

Acknowledge previous interactions in ways that demonstrate understanding and continuity. *"Your team's engagement with our operational excellence resources suggests you might find value in our upcoming implementation workshop"* shows attention to recipient interests while suggesting relevant next steps.

Value-Based Progression

Focus on creating clear value at each interaction level. Whether through knowledge sharing, problem-solving tools, or strategic insights, ensure each engagement point delivers meaningful benefit while building toward deeper partnership opportunities.

Remember that relationship development should flow naturally from delivered value rather than prescribed steps. Focus on creating genuine opportunities for engagement that align with recipient needs and interests.

The goal is to build strong professional relationships through consistent value delivery and natural progression rather than predetermined paths.

Moving forward, let's explore how automation and personalization enhances these relationship-building efforts while maintaining authentic engagement.

Automation and Personalization

Email marketing demands both efficiency and authenticity. While automation helps us maintain consistent communication at scale, the personal touch remains crucial for building meaningful business relationships. The key lies in finding the right balance between technological capability and human connection.

Trigger-Based Emails: Right Message, Right Time

Think of modern email automation as your always-alert business development team. It notices important moments and responds appropriately - whether that's welcoming new subscribers, following up on interactions, or reaching out when engagement patterns shift. This systematic approach ensures that no important opportunity for connection slips through the cracks.

Key Engagement Moments

Several critical points in the customer journey benefit from immediate, relevant response:

When someone joins your community, a thoughtfully designed welcome sequence introduces them to your value proposition and begins building relationship foundations. After significant interactions and purchases, timely follow-up with relevant resources and support enhances experience and demonstrates attention to their needs.

If engagement patterns change - perhaps someone hasn't opened recent communications - automated re-engagement sequences help renew the connection. Similarly, recognizing important milestones or achievements helps maintain relationship strength through acknowledgment of significant moments.

Success requires understanding your audience's typical journey and identifying moments where automated communication provides genuine value. Map out these critical points and design responses that appear natural while addressing real needs or interests.

Behavioral Segmentation: Because Actions Speak Louder Than Words

Behavioral segmentation in email marketing means dividing your audience based on their actions. Instead of treating everyone the same, people are grouped based on what they do—such as which emails they open, what links they click, or how often they buy something. By analyzing behavioral patterns, we are able to create relevant, engaging communications that respond to demonstrated interests and needs.

Engagement Analysis

Different recipients interact with your communications in distinct ways. Some consistently engage with detailed technical content, while others focus on strategic insights or implementation guidance. Understanding these patterns helps tailor future communications more effectively.

Interaction Tracking

Whether through website visits, content downloads, or email engagement, recipient behavior provides valuable insight into interests and needs. When someone repeatedly explores specific topics or solutions, this indicates areas where deeper or more specialized content could be valuable.

Purchase Pattern Recognition

Previous purchasing decisions often indicate future interests or needs. Understanding these patterns helps identify relevant additional solutions and complementary offerings that are likely to provide value to the recipients.

Content Preference Patterns

By monitoring which topics, formats, or approaches generate the strongest engagement, we have the ability to refine our communication strategy for specific audience segments. This might mean sending more technical detail to some recipients while focusing on strategic overview for others.

This understanding enables nuanced, relevant communication. For example, when we observe ongoing interest in specific topics or solutions, we can proactively offer related insights or resources: *"Based on your interest in operational efficiency, we thought you'd find value in our latest implementation framework."*

Dynamic Content: One Email, Many Versions

Different subscribers see different versions of an email based on their interests or actions. Instead of sending the same email to everyone, personalizing sections like images, text, or offers for each person is effective. For example, if one subscriber likes shoes and another subscriber likes bags, each will see content related to what they like most. This makes your emails relevant, leading to better engagement.

Contextual Content Delivery

Emails become impactful when they reflect recipient-specific contexts. Whether adjusting case studies based on industry focus, modifying solution descriptions for different organization sizes, or tailoring implementation examples to specific sectors, this targeted approach ensures maximum relevance.

Situational Customization

Geographic location, organizational role, and industry sector often influence which information proves most valuable. By incorporating these factors into our content strategy, each recipient receives the most pertinent information for their situation. For instance, regional event details, local implementation examples, and sector-specific benchmarks can automatically adjust based on recipient profiles.

Experience-Based Messaging

Different relationship stages often require different approaches. Long-term clients might receive more advanced insights or exclusive offerings, while newer relationships focus on fundamental value propositions. This automatic adjustment ensures appropriate messaging without creating multiple campaigns.

The goal is to deliver precisely relevant information to each recipient while maintaining efficient communication operations. This ensures maximum impact while optimizing resource utilization.

Personalization Beyond {FirstName}

Basic name insertion barely scratches the surface of true personalization. Creating genuinely relevant communications requires deeper understanding and acknowledgment of the recipients' experiences, preferences, and objectives.

Engagement Recognition

Acknowledge your shared history in meaningful ways. Rather than simply noting how long someone has been connected with your organization, reference specific interactions or value they've found. "Following your successful implementation last quarter..." creates a stronger authentic connection than generic anniversaries.

Context Awareness

Show understanding of the reader's specific situation. If they have recently adopted a new solution or started a particular initiative, reference this context in your communications. "As you continue developing your automation strategy..." feels more relevant than generic messaging.

Language Alignment

Pay attention to how your recipients describe their challenges and objectives. Using their terminology and framing in your communications shows genuine understanding, creating natural rapport. This might mean adjusting technical terms, industry references, or process descriptions to match their preferences.

Goal-Based Communication

Focus on the recipient's objectives rather than your products or services. When you understand what someone is working to achieve, you are then able to frame communications around their goals: "Based on your focus on operational efficiency..." This approach demonstrates partnership rather than just vendor relationship.

Effective personalization demonstrates understanding without overstepping professional boundaries. The goal is creating relevant, valuable communications that acknowledge individual context while maintaining appropriate business relationships.

Automation Workflows: Building Your Email Marketing Machine

Think of email sequences as akin to a conversation that develops naturally over time. Just as you would avoid telling someone everything about your business in the first meeting, your emails ought to gradually build understanding and engagement.

Creating Your Sequence

Start by planning how you want relationships to develop. What should people learn first? What questions will they have along the way? How do they typically move from interest to engagement to action? Map out these steps to create a natural progression.

Key Moments

Identify important points that trigger specific messages:

- When an individual initially connects with your organization
- After they show interest in particular topics
- When they take specific actions
- If they haven't engaged for a while

Message Development

Create content matching each stage of the relationship. Early messages focus on sharing helpful insights and building credibility. Later ones introduce specific solutions or opportunities as interest develops.

Natural Progression

A typical sequence could flow like this:
- Welcome and orientation
- Helpful insights and resources
- Initial solution exploration
- Specific opportunity discussion
- Implementation support
- Additional value opportunities

Remember to monitor how people engage with your sequence and adjust this based on what you learn. The goal is to create a flow of communications that feels natural and helpful rather than automated and pushy.

The Human Touch in Automation: Keeping It Real

While automation helps us stay consistent and efficient, keeping communications genuine and personal remains essential. The goal is using technology to enhance rather than replace real human connection.

Natural Communication Style

Write your messages the way you'd speak in a professional conversation. Instead of formal, stilted language, use a natural tone that builds rapport while maintaining professionalism. Share relevant experiences and insights that help recipients relate to your message.

Creating Real Dialogue

Encourage conversation rather than one-way communication. Ask thoughtful questions about challenges or objectives. Make it clear that you welcome replies and discussion. When people respond, ensure they receive prompt, personal attention.

Adding Personal Elements

Look for opportunities to acknowledge individual situations and experiences. Reference specific challenges they've mentioned or goals they're pursuing. Share relevant case studies or examples that relate directly to their context.

Unexpected Touchpoints

Occasionally step outside the automated sequence to add personal notes or share particularly relevant insights. These unscheduled touchpoints maintain authentic connection within the structured communication flow.

Regular Review

Periodically review automated messages, ensuring they remain current and appropriate. Industry changes, new challenges, and shifting priorities require adjustments to keep communications relevant and valuable.

Technology serves to support rather than replace personal connection. Focus on using automation to deliver consistently valuable communications while maintaining authentic, professional relationships.

Compliance and Best Practices

Staying on the Right Side of the Law (and Your Subscribers)

To stay compliant, it is imperative that email marketing follows legal requirements and best practices. Beyond legal obligations, we have a personal responsibility to treat subscribers ethically. It's important for businesses to understand these rules not only to avoid penalties but also to build genuine trust with our audience.

While these regulations might seem complex, their goal is simple: protect recipients' privacy while allowing legitimate business communication. By following these guidelines, businesses build strong relationships with their audience, gain credibility, and make their marketing more effective.

Several major regulations govern email marketing across different regions:

European Union (GDPR)

When communicating with European residents, you must obtain clear consent to use their data. Recipients need to actively agree to receive your emails, and they have the right to access or remove their information at any time.

United States (CAN-SPAM)

U.S. regulations emphasize transparency. Your emails must:

- Clearly identify themselves as marketing communications
- Use honest subject lines
- Include your business address
- Provide an easy way for recipients to unsubscribe

Canada (CASL)

Canadian rules focus on consent and clarity. You need either explicit permission or an existing business relationship to send marketing emails. Similar to other regulations, you must clearly identify yourself and offer a simple unsubscribe option.

Practical Implementation

While specific requirements vary by region, following these general principles will help you stay compliant:

- Obtain clear consent before sending marketing emails
- Be transparent about your identity and purpose
- Make opting out easy and accessible
- Maintain thorough records of permissions and preferences
- Respond promptly to unsubscribe requests

These regulations protect both senders and recipients by preserving trust in email communications. If you're unsure about specific requirements, consulting a legal professional can help to ensure full compliance.

Double Opt-In: The Gold Standard of Consent

Double opt-in is a process requiring subscribers to confirm their interest twice. First, they sign up for your email list, and then they receive a follow-up email where they must click a link to confirm their subscription.

While single opt-in might be simpler, double opt-in takes your email list security to the next level by ensuring that every subscriber is genuinely interested and committed to receiving your emails.

This method emphasizes verifying intent and prioritizes quality over quantity, meaning your list consists of people who truly want to be there.

How it works

When an individual signs up for your email list, they receive a follow-up email asking them to confirm their subscription by clicking a link. This extra step ensures the email address is valid and that the subscriber genuinely wants to hear from you.

Benefits

Confirms genuine interest from subscribers: With double opt-in, you know your subscribers are genuinely interested in your content because they took the extra step to confirm their subscription.

Reduces the chances of spam complaints: By confirming their intent, subscribers are less likely to mark your emails as spam, which helps maintain a good sender reputation.

Boosts email deliverability: Email providers assess engagement levels to decide whether your emails land in the inbox or the spam folder. Double opt-in helps ensure a more engaged list, which improves deliverability and increase the likelihood of your emails reaching your audience.

Helps meet stricter regulations like GDPR: Regulations such as GDPR require proof of consent; double opt-in provides that. Keeping records of subscribers' confirmation helps ensure compliance and avoid potential legal issues.

Improves list quality: Since only interested subscribers complete the double opt-in process, you end up with a higher-quality list of engaged users who are more likely to open your emails, click on your links, and make a purchase.

Reduces fake sign-ups: Double opt-in acts as a filter for fake or mistyped email addresses. Since subscribers need to verify their email, you're less likely to end up with invalid addresses or bots on your list.

Example email

"Hey there! We're thrilled you want to join our awesome email club. Just click the link below to confirm and let the email magic begin! We can't wait to start sharing our best content, tips, and exclusive offers with you. Confirm now and be part of something great!"

List Hygiene: Keeping Your Email List Squeaky Clean

A clean email list is a healthy email list. Keeping your list in top shape is crucial for effective email marketing, as it helps maintain good deliverability rates, ensures that your emails are reaching engaged subscribers, and ultimately improves your campaign's overall performance. Here's how to keep yours in top shape:

Remove hard bounces regularly

Hard bounces happen when an email address doesn't exist anymore, often due to typos during sign-up, someone changing their email provider, or a domain no longer being active. It's important to remove these addresses promptly to keep your list accurate and prevent harming your sender reputation.

Keep an eye on soft bounces

Soft bounces occur due to temporary issues, like a full inbox or server problems. It's okay to keep these subscribers for a while, but if an address keeps bouncing repeatedly, it may indicate an issue that won't be resolved, and it's best to remove it from your list to maintain quality.

Avoid spam traps

Spam traps are fake email addresses used by internet service providers (ISPs) and anti-spam organizations to identify senders with poor list management practices. If you accidentally hit a spam trap, it may significantly damage your sender reputation. To avoid this, regularly clean your list, never buy email lists, and ensure that all your subscribers have genuinely opted in.

Set a sunset policy

Subscribers who haven't opened or clicked any of your emails for a certain number of months are unlikely to suddenly start engaging again. Set a timeframe, such as six months, to determine when to remove inactive subscribers from your list. Focusing on active users improves engagement rates and maintains a high-quality list.

Run re-engagement campaigns

Before removing inactive subscribers, it's a good idea to give them a few last chances to re-engage. Send a re-engagement campaign with special offers, exclusive content, or a heartfelt message asking if they still want to hear from you. This way, you can win back inactive subscribers while also confirming who's genuinely interested.

Segment your list for better results

Regular list cleaning gives you the chance to segment subscribers based on activity levels. Engaged subscribers receive your most important campaigns, while inactive users are targeted with re-engagement efforts. This segmentation helps improve the relevance of content, leading to higher open rates and conversions.

Regularly validate email addresses

Even when people sign up willingly, there's always the risk of typos or fake addresses being submitted. Use an email validation service to identify and remove invalid addresses to keep your list accurate and reduce bounce rates.

Always remember, when it comes to email lists, quality is more important than quantity. A smaller list full of engaged, interested subscribers outperforms a large list of unengaged, inactive contacts. Focus on keeping the list clean and populated with people who genuinely want to receive your content, and your email marketing efforts will be far more successful.

Managing Unsubscribes and Preferences

Nobody likes a clingy ex. Make it easy for subscribers to leave or take a break if they need to:

One-click unsubscribe

Make it easy for people to unsubscribe. A single click should be enough to opt out. The easier you make it for someone to leave, the more likely they are to trust you in the future, and they could even resubscribe later if they feel comfortable.

Honor unsubscribes promptly

The law usually requires you to process unsubscribes within 10 business days, however, doing it sooner is better. Promptly removing people from your list shows respect for their preferences, helping maintain your brand's reputation. When subscribers see that you act quickly, it builds trust and reduces frustration.

Offer alternatives

Instead of fully unsubscribing, give subscribers options to change how often they hear from you or what type of content they receive. Some subscribers might simply feel overwhelmed by too many emails. Offering different frequency options (such as weekly instead of daily) or allowing them to choose specific topics they care about can help retain them.

Keep the unsubscribe link visible

Make sure the unsubscribe link is easy to find. Don't hide it—it should be clear and accessible. People appreciate transparency, and making the link obvious reduces their frustration if they decide to opt out. A visible unsubscribe link shows respect for their choice, which reflects positively on your brand.

Ask for feedback

A quick 'Why are you leaving?' survey may provide useful insights to help you improve. Understanding why subscribers are opting out reveals patterns, such as content that isn't resonating or an email frequency that is too high. Keep the survey short and optional—one or two questions are enough to gather valuable information without making it a burden for the person leaving. Use the feedback to make meaningful changes to your email strategy.

Remind subscribers they can come back anytime

Let subscribers know that they are always welcome to resubscribe in the future. A friendly message indicating they can return when they are ready keeps the door open and leaves a positive impression of your brand.

Example Email

"We're sad to see you go! Before you leave, would you like to receive fewer emails instead? If you decide to leave now, remember, you're always welcome back—we'd love to have you!"

Privacy and Data Protection: Treating Subscriber Data Like Fort Knox

Your subscribers' data is extremely valuable, and as a business, you have a duty of care to protect it at all costs. This means handling their information with the highest level of respect and responsibility. Your subscribers trust you to keep their data safe, and it is your obligation to honor that trust by taking all necessary precautions. Protecting subscriber data isn't only a matter of compliance—it demonstrates that you genuinely care for their privacy and well-being:

Be clear about data collection

Explain exactly what data you're collecting and why. Transparency builds trust, making subscribers more comfortable sharing their information. You can do this by including clear explanations on your sign-up forms and providing easy-to-understand details in your privacy policy. When subscribers understand what data that you collect and how it benefits them, they are more likely to engage positively with your brand.

Keep data secure

Store data safely by using encryption and limiting who can access it. Protecting personal information is key to maintaining your subscribers' trust. Make sure you are using up-to-date security measures, such as SSL encryption, regularly auditing data storage processes to identify potential vulnerabilities. Additionally, train your team on data protection best practices to minimize risks of accidental data breaches.

Never share or sell email lists

Sharing or selling your email list is not only unethical but often illegal. Respect your subscribers' privacy and keep their information to yourself. Your subscribers trust you with their personal information and betraying that trust can lead to significant legal consequences and damage to your brand reputation. Instead, focus on building genuine relationships with your audience and offering value through your own marketing efforts.

Keep your privacy policy updated

Make sure your privacy policy is accurate and reflects how you handle subscriber data. This shows you take privacy seriously.

Review your privacy policy regularly, especially if you make changes to how you collect or use data. Keeping it up to date helps ensure compliance with relevant regulations and gives subscribers confidence that their data is in safe hands. Make your privacy policy is easy to find and understand, so subscribers know exactly what to expect.

Be ready for data requests

Under regulations like GDPR, subscribers have the right to ask for their data. Be prepared to provide it if needed, handling these requests promptly and professionally. Create a clear process for handling data requests, including verifying the identity of the requester to ensure their data is protected. Responding quickly and respectfully to data requests demonstrates to your subscribers that you value their rights and take data protection seriously. This helps build long-term trust and loyalty with your audience.

Regularly review and audit your data practices

In addition to the points above, it's important to regularly review and audit how you collect, store, and use subscriber data. Conducting regular audits helps identify areas for improvement and ensures that you remain compliant with privacy regulations. Staying proactive about data protection aids in preventing potential issues before they arise, safeguarding both your brand and your subscribers.

Always remember, subscriber data is a responsibility, not just an asset. By treating it with the care it deserves, you build trust, protect your brand, and create meaningful, long-lasting relationships with your audience.

Deliverability Best Practices: Staying Out of the Spam Folder

All your hard work has the potential to go to waste if your emails fail to reach your subscribers' inboxes. Deliverability is one of the most important aspects of email marketing, as it determines whether your carefully crafted messages will even be seen. Ensuring emails make it to the inbox involves more than just hitting 'send'; it requires understanding how to navigate spam filters, build trust with email service providers, and engage your audience effectively. Here are some practical steps you can take to improve your deliverability:

Authenticate emails

Use authentication protocols such as SPF, DKIM, and DMARC to prove that your emails are legitimate. This helps prevent your emails from being marked as spam and increases the likelihood that they will reach the intended recipients. Authentication builds credibility with email service providers, which is crucial for maintaining a good sender reputation. If this sounds too technical, don't worry—your tech team or email provider should be able to assist you in setting this up.

Maintain a good sender reputation

Keep engagement rates high and complaints low. Ensure emails are relevant, interesting, and valuable to your subscribers to encourage them to open and interact with your messages. A good sender reputation is built by consistently sending quality content that your audience wants. Avoid frequent complaints or spam reports by staying focused on providing real value.

Avoid spammy words

Words like "Free," "Guarantee," or "No obligation" can trigger spam filters. Choose your language carefully to keep your emails looking trustworthy. Instead of relying on overused and salesy words, make your subject lines and content more conversational and personal. Focus on language that resonates with the audience and addresses their needs without sounding pushy.

Balance text and images

Too many images can make your email look suspicious to spam filters. Make sure you have a good mix of text and images to avoid any issues. It's a good idea to use descriptive text along with images so that subscribers can still understand the message even if images don't load. A balanced approach makes emails appealing and prevents them from getting flagged.

Warm up new IP addresses

If you're using a new IP to send emails, start by sending smaller volumes and gradually increase. This helps build a good reputation with email providers. Warming up an IP address slowly signals to email service providers that your email activity is legitimate, which improves deliverability over time. Being patient and consistent establishes a positive sender reputation from the start.

Send emails at optimal times

Timing plays a big role in deliverability. Research when your audience is most likely to be online and engaged, then send your emails at random times during those peak periods. This can boost open rates and overall engagement, helping improve your reputation as a sender.

Use a consistent sending schedule

Sending emails at consistent intervals builds trust with both your subscribers and email service providers. A predictable schedule helps your audience know when to expect your messages, which can increase engagement. Avoid sending emails too infrequently, which can lead to subscribers forgetting about you, or too frequently, which may cause annoyance.

Personalize content

Personalized emails often perform better in terms of engagement. Include the recipient's name and tailor the content to their preferences or previous interactions. Personalization makes emails feel relevant, which increases the chances that they will be opened and engaged with, improving your sender reputation.

Monitor metrics

Keep an eye on key performance metrics such as open rates, click-through rates, and bounce rates. These metrics give you insights into how well your campaigns are performing and how email providers view your emails. If your metrics start to decline, it may be time to adjust your content or list practices to improve deliverability.

Following these best practices isn't just about staying out of trouble—it's about respecting your subscribers and building trust with them. In email marketing, trust is everything. When subscribers know they can expect valuable, relevant, and respectful content, they are far more likely to engage positively.

Now that you're equipped with the essentials of compliance and best practices, you're ready to create email nurture sequences that are not only effective, but also ethical and respectful. In our final section, we'll dive into some advanced techniques to take your email marketing to the next level. Stay tuned, email marketing expert!

Advanced Techniques

Taking Your Email Game to the Next Level

Alright, you've got the basics down and you're following best practices like a pro. Now it's time to take things up a notch, adding advanced techniques to your email marketing toolkit. Let's explore some strategies that will leave your subscribers thinking, "Wow, this is impressive!"

Interactive Emails: Bringing the Web to the Inbox

Why make your subscribers click a link to visit your website when they can engage directly from their inbox? Here are some ways to make emails interactive and engaging:

AMP for Email

AMP (Accelerated Mobile Pages) for email allows you to create dynamic, interactive experiences directly within the email. It enables users to interact with content—like filling out forms or viewing updated product details—without ever leaving their inbox.

Include live content that updates in real time, such as product availability, countdown timers, or latest blog posts. This keeps subscribers informed without needing to click away.

Add interactive forms to allow subscribers to respond without leaving the email. Include elements like survey questions, appointment bookings, or quick polls to make engagement seamless and easy.

Using accordion features to present information in a compact, easy-to-navigate way—such as FAQs or step-by-step guides—allows users to expand and view only the content they are interested in.

Cascading Style Sheets (CSS) Animations

CSS animations are small, scripted movements that enhance elements in your emails, making them more visually appealing and engaging. They draw attention to key parts of your message, like animated buttons or icons that guide subscribers to important actions or create a sense of excitement.

Use subtle animations for CTA buttons, making them stand out without being overwhelming.

Animations can highlight new products or services, catching the reader's eye and encouraging interaction.

Rollover Effects

Use rollover effects to change images or text, adding a fun, interactive touch that keeps subscribers engaged. This makes your emails dynamic and creates a sense of discovery for the reader.

For product showcases, use rollover effects to display different angles or colors when subscribers hover over an image, providing an immersive shopping experience.

Text rollovers can be used to reveal more details or descriptions, adding an interactive layer to email content that encourages exploration.

Embedded Videos

Let subscribers watch videos without leaving their inbox, simplifying interaction with your content. Videos can be used to tell a story, demonstrate a product, or share a message in an engaging way.

Use videos to offer a behind-the-scenes look at your business, introduce new products, or share customer testimonials to build trust.

Adding a play button overlay on a video thumbnail can spark curiosity, drive more clicks, and increase the likelihood that your content will be viewed.

Countdown Timers

Incorporate countdown timers for limited time offers or upcoming events. This creates a sense of urgency and encourages subscribers to take action before time runs out.

Use countdown timers to highlight flash sales, event registrations, and limited-time discounts, ensuring your email feels immediate and actionable.

Timers add a dynamic element to your emails, giving them an up-to-date and timely feel.

Pro tip: Always have a backup plan for subscribers using email clients that don't support these features. Since not everyone will see interactive elements, ensure your email still functions well for all recipients. Include alternative text or fallback content to create a positive experience for all subscribers, regardless of their email client.

Gamification in Email Marketing: Let's Play!

Who says emails can't be fun? Adding gamification elements can make your emails engaging and help your brand stand out. By incorporating fun and interactive elements, you not only increase engagement but also create a memorable experience that encourages subscribers to look forward to your messages. Here are some simple but effective ways to make your emails interactive and exciting:

Spin-to-win

Give subscribers the chance to spin a virtual wheel for a prize or discount. This creates excitement and encourages them to interact with your email. The anticipation of winning something keeps subscribers engaged, and the interactive nature of a spinning wheel adds a sense of playfulness. You could use it to offer different types of rewards like discounts, free products, or even exclusive content.

Puzzles or riddles

Include puzzles or riddles to engage your subscribers' problem-solving skills, creating a memorable experience and encouraging them to spend more time on your email. Adding a challenge, like a trivia question or a riddle, prompts subscribers to think and have fun simultaneously. You can even reward correct answers with discounts or exclusive offers, enhancing the experience and adding a rewarding touch.

Progress bars

Show subscribers how close they are to earning a reward such as a discount or freebie. Progress bars motivate people to keep engaging with your content. They give a sense of achievement and encourage continued interaction. For example, you could show how many more points they need to earn a reward, which can drive repeat engagement and encourage subscribers to become invested in your emails.

Points systems

Reward subscribers for engaging with your emails by giving them points to redeem for perks. This encourages them to stay involved and interact more often. A points-based loyalty program drives consistent engagement, as subscribers will be motivated to collect points by opening emails, clicking links, or making purchases. It creates a sense of progress and incentivizes people to keep interacting with your brand.

Interactive quizzes

Include fun quizzes that allow subscribers to learn something new about themselves or your products. Quizzes can recommend products based on a subscriber's answers or educate them on a topic. The more engaging the quiz, the more likely they are to share the results or revisit your brand.

Badges and achievements

Create digital badges or achievements that are earned by interacting with your content. These badges can be used to signify milestones, such as being subscribed for a certain period or completing challenges in your emails. Recognizing subscribers' efforts builds loyalty and ensures they feel valued.

Example: *"Solve this riddle to unlock your special discount code! What has keys but no locks, space but no room, and you can enter but not go in?"*

Gamification in email marketing isn't just about making emails more fun; it's also about creating a stronger connection with your subscribers. These techniques can help your content be more interactive, enjoyable, and memorable, ultimately leading to better engagement and customer loyalty. Try adding some of these elements to your next campaign and watch how your subscribers respond!

By the way, if you are dying to know the answer to that riddle......it's a keyboard!

Integrating Email with Other Channels: Breaking Down the Silos

Email shouldn't work alone. To create a smooth and consistent experience for your audience, it is essential to connect email with other channels. When all of your marketing channels work together, they create a seamless journey for your audience, making them more likely to engage and take action. Here are some effective ways to make your marketing cohesive:

Social media integration

Share email content on social media or use social content in your emails. This approach reaches a wider audience and keeps messaging consistent across platforms. Encourage subscribers to share your email content on their social channels, increasing your reach even further. Adding social share buttons in your emails makes it easy for your audience to spread the word.

SMS follow-ups

Send text messages to remind subscribers about important emails or promotions. SMS follow-ups can help ensure they don't miss out on key offers or updates. SMS is great for urgent or time-sensitive messages, such as flash sales or event reminders. It complements email well by providing an extra nudge to your audience. Using SMS in tandem with email creates multiple touchpoints that improves overall engagement.

Retargeting ads

Show targeted ads to subscribers who failed to engage with specific emails. This keeps your message in front of them, giving another opportunity to take action. Retargeting ads reinforce the content of your email and remind subscribers of what they might be missing. For example, if someone opened your email but didn't click through, retargeting ads can encourage them to come back and complete the action. This additional exposure is a powerful way to drive conversions.

Direct mail integration

For high-value prospects, follow up on your emails with physical mailers. Combining digital and physical touchpoints make a big impact and help your brand stand out. Direct mail feels personal and tangible, making it a great complement to email. Sending a personalized postcard or a brochure to someone who has shown interest in your emails creates a deeper connection and can move them further down the sales funnel.

Website personalization

Integrate email campaigns with your website by using personalization. When subscribers click through from an email, ensure they land on a page that reflects what they saw in the email. Personalized landing pages create a consistent experience and make it more likely that users will convert. Use dynamic content to tailor website messaging based on actions subscribers took in your emails.

Cross-channel analytics

Track your audience's journey across multiple channels to see how email interacts with other touchpoints. Use analytics to understand which channels are driving the most engagement and how they influence one another. This will help you optimize your overall marketing strategy and ensure that each channel is supporting the others effectively.

The goal is to create a consistent experience across all channels so that your audience feels connected, no matter how they interact with your brand. Breaking down the silos and integrating email marketing with other channels creates a unified approach that delivers value at every touchpoint, ultimately building stronger relationships with your audience.

User-Generated Content (UGC) in Emails: Let Your Customers Do the Talking

Nothing builds trust like hearing directly from satisfied customers. Adding UGC to emails enhances their relatability and trustworthiness. Including authentic content from real users creates a personal connection and enhances the effectiveness of emails. Here are some easy ways to include UGC:

Customer reviews

Include glowing customer reviews in your emails to showcase what people love about your product. This builds credibility and reassures new subscribers. Featuring real testimonials helps potential customers feel more confident about choosing your product, as they see that others have had a great experience.

Social media posts

Highlight social media posts from customers using your product. Sharing real experiences from customers makes your brand feel authentic and encourages others to join in. You can use posts from

Instagram, Facebook, or Twitter, showing how real people are interacting with your brand in their everyday lives. Including customer photos or quotes makes your emails more engaging and relatable.

Customer stories

Share detailed success stories and case studies from customers. These stories can demonstrate how your product made a difference, helping potential customers envision how it could work for them too. Whether it's a story about achieving a goal, solving a problem, or transforming a situation, detailed customer stories create a narrative that resonates emotionally with your audience and can inspire them to take action.

Polls and surveys

Ask customers for their opinions and feature the results in your emails. Polls and surveys are great ways to gather feedback while also making subscribers feel heard. Featuring the results in your emails shows that you value your audience's input and can help shape future products or services.

Pro tip: Always get permission from customers before using their content in your emails! It's important to respect their privacy and make sure they're comfortable with their content being shared.

These advanced techniques are tools to add to your email marketing toolbox. Not every approach will be right for every campaign, so the key is to experiment and learn. Keep your subscribers' needs and preferences at the center of your efforts. Test different approaches, see what resonates best with your audience, and adjust accordingly to keep improving your emails.

Where to From Here (and How to Stay Ahead of the Curve)

We've reached the end of our journey through the world of email nurture sequences. But remember, every ending is just the start of something new. Let's recap what we've learned and take a quick look at what lies ahead in the constantly changing world of email marketing.

Email marketing is always evolving, and staying ahead requires continuous learning and adapting to new trends. To truly excel, you need to not only understand the current best practices but also be prepared to innovate. This involves staying up to date with the latest developments, experimenting with new strategies, and consistently focusing on delivering the best possible experience for your subscribers. Email marketing is about building and nurturing relationships, requiring responsiveness to change and a willingness to grow.

Key Takeaways

Let us take a moment to revisit some of the key lessons throughout the book:

Know your audience

Personalization is crucial, starting with understanding your subscribers. Take the time to gather insights about their preferences, behavior, and needs. The more you know about your audience, the more effectively you're able to tailor content to meet expectations.

Provide value

Ensure every email gives the subscriber a reason to be glad they opened it. Whether it's useful information, a special offer, or exclusive content, always think about how to provide real value and improve the subscriber experience.

Respect your subscribers

Follow best practices and regulations to build trust and keep a good reputation. Respecting subscribers means honoring their preferences, being transparent about how you use their data, and making it easy for them to manage their subscription.

Think beyond email

Connect your email strategy with other marketing channels, creating a seamless experience. Whether it's social media, SMS, or direct mail, integrating email campaigns with other channels ensures a consistent and unified message that reaches your audience wherever they are.

Automate wisely

Use automation to send timely, relevant emails, but don't lose the personal touch. Automation can help deliver the right message at the right time, however, it's important that emails feel personal and genuine. It is important for automation to enhance, not replace, the human element of your emails.

Design for all devices

With mobile being so popular, make sure your emails look great on every device. Responsive design is non-negotiable, and ensuring your emails are easy to read and interact with on any screen size is crucial for engagement. Test emails on multiple devices to guarantee they provide a great experience for everyone.

Craft compelling content

From subject lines to CTAs, every word matters. The content

should be engaging, concise, and focused on encouraging your subscribers to take action. A great subject line has the ability to make the difference between an email that gets opened and one that gets ignored, so take the time to craft messages that resonate.

Stay human

Remember, there's a real person at the other end of each email, so keep your messages personal and genuine. Avoid sounding overly robotic or salesy. Use conversational language, address your subscribers by name, and show empathy. Building a connection with your audience is what sets successful email marketers apart.

The future of email marketing is always evolving. By staying adaptable, putting subscribers first, and continuing to learn, you'll be well-prepared to keep your email campaigns ahead of the curve.

Staying Ahead of the Curve: Your Email Marketing Growth Plan

Before I sign off, I want to leave you with this: with so many exciting changes happening in email marketing, staying ahead of the competition can appear challenging, but it's also an opportunity for growth. The industry is constantly evolving, and keeping up can be the key to success. Here are some practical and effective tips to help you stay ahead and continue to grow:

Keep learning

Stay up to date by following industry blogs, attending webinars, and joining email marketing communities. There's always something new to learn. Consider taking online courses or obtaining certifications to deepen your knowledge. Staying informed will keep you ahead of the curve and help you apply the latest tactics to your campaigns.

Experiment regularly

Set aside time and resources to try out new technologies and strategies. When you test different approaches, you discover what works best for your audience. Try A/B testing subject lines, experimenting with different content formats, and using new tools to ascertain what resonates with your subscribers. Remember, experimentation is key to discovering creative solutions and staying innovative.

Listen to your subscribers

Your subscribers are your best source of feedback. Pay attention to their responses and adjust your approach based on what they like and don't like. Use surveys, polls, or even direct feedback to get a sense of what your audience values. Keeping an open line of communication ensures that your emails meet their needs and keeps them engaged.

Stay flexible

Be ready to adjust your strategy as new trends and technologies emerge. The email marketing world changes fast and staying adaptable will keep you ahead. Whether it's incorporating new automation tools, adjusting to changing privacy regulations, or adopting fresh content formats, flexibility is crucial for maintaining relevance and effectiveness.

Focus on the basics

While it's great to explore new trends, don't forget the fundamentals of good email marketing—relevant content, personalization, and respect for your subscribers. Consistency in these basics builds a strong foundation for success. Always keep in mind that great email marketing starts with understanding your audience and delivering valuable content.

Stay on top of regulations

Keep informed about changes in privacy laws and email regulations. Staying compliant is key to maintaining your subscribers' trust. Regulations such as GDPR and CAN-SPAM are constantly evolving, and staying aware of these changes is essential. It's not just about avoiding penalties; it's about building long-lasting trust with your audience by respecting their privacy.

Track your performance

Make sure to measure the performance of your email campaigns regularly. Use metrics like open rates, click-through rates, and conversions to understand what's working and where there's room for improvement. Regular analysis helps refine your approach, making your campaigns more effective over time.

Stay creative and inspired

Don't be afraid to try new things and think outside the box. Creativity in email marketing gives you an edge when it comes to standing out from the competition and capturing your subscribers' attention. Take inspiration from successful campaigns you've seen or draw ideas from other industries. A creative mindset makes your emails engaging and memorable.

The future of email marketing is full of opportunities, but it can also be challenging. The key to success is balancing new technology with the timeless principles of good communication and respect for your audience. Always keep learning, stay flexible, and focus on delivering value to your subscribers.

And there you have it! You're now equipped with everything you need to succeed in email marketing—from the basics to advanced techniques, real-world examples, and future trends. The world of email marketing is open to you, and we can't wait to see what you create.

So go ahead and conquer those inboxes! Your subscribers are ready for your next amazing email nurture sequence. Happy emailing!

About the Author

Vince Warnock is an award-winning marketing and visibility coach, best-selling author and host of the Chasing the Insights podcast.

An ex-radio announcer with 20+ years in marketing, Vince was previously the Chief Marketing Officer at Cigna Insurance and has founded and sold multiple companies, including high-growth tech start-up Common Ledger.

Vince is the founder of ATG Publishing, Business Mind Magazine and the Chasing the Insights podcast, where he empowers entrepreneurs and business owners to get seen, get published, and position themselves as the thought leader that they are.

Vince's work has received numerous awards from his peers, highlighting his notable achievements. Among these is being named as part of the Fearless50, a program created by Adobe/Marketo. This prestigious recognition is given to the top 50 digital marketers in the world who are known for driving bold, fearless marketing and digital transformation.

He is consistently challenging the industry to adopt a duty-of-care mentality when it comes to marketing. Not just with security and privacy, but also with messaging to ensure that each of us are in no way manipulating or misleading our audiences or potential clients.

You will find multiple ways to connect with Vince at https://chasingtheinsights.com

More Books by Vince Warnock

Vince's goal is to empower one million entrepreneurs to grow an impacting and profitable business that makes them proud.

One of the ways Vince is going to achieve this is through the many books he authors.

Check out the range of other titles on the Chasing the Insights website.

https://chasingtheinsights.com/books/